Republic of Iraq
Public Expenditure Review

A WORLD BANK STUDY

Republic of Iraq
Public Expenditure Review

Toward More Efficient Spending
for Better Service Delivery

WORLD BANK GROUP
Washington, D.C.

Contents

Box

Figures

Tables

Acknowledgments

This report was written by a team led by Sibel Kulaksiz (Task Team Leader and Senior Country Economist) and composed of Ibrahim Al-Ghelaiqah (Senior Economist), Simon Stolp (Senior Energy Specialist), Ferhat Esen (Senior Energy Specialist), Bjorn Ekman (Senior Health Economist), and Andrew Laing (Consultant). Valuable input and feedback were received from Abebe Adugna Dadi (Lead Economist), Kevin Carey (Lead Economist), Husam Beides (Lead Energy Specialist), Janet Dooley (Senior Country Officer), Ghassan Alkhoja (Senior Operations Officer), Montserrat Pallares-Millares (Social Protection Specialist), Peter Muir (Consultant), Francisco Parodi (Senior Economist, International Monetary Fund), and Koralai Kirabaeva (Economist, International Monetary Fund). The report was prepared under the guidance of Jorge Araujo (Lead Economist) and the supervision of Manuela V. Ferro (Sector Director) and Bernard G. Funck (Sector Manager). Hedi Larbi (former Country Director) and Marie-Hélène Bricknell (Special Representative for Iraq) provided advice and guidance. Special gratitude is due to Inger Andersen (Vice President, Middle East and North Africa Region) and Ferid Belhaj (Director, Middle East Department).

The peer reviewers for this report are Ivailo Izvorski (Sector Manager), Tracey Lane (Senior Economist), and Kai Kaiser (Senior Economist). Additional useful comments were received from Caroline van den Berg (Lead Water and Sanitation Specialist), Arun Arya (Senior Public Sector Management Specialist), Mona El Chami (Senior Financial Management Specialist), Ousman Jah (Senior Operations Officer), and Ron Van Rooden (Mission Chief for Iraq, International Monetary Fund). Syviengxay Creger and Muna Abeid Salim edited the report.

The team is grateful for the close and productive cooperation of the Iraqi counterparts during the preparation of this report. This work is a product of the staff of the World Bank. The findings, interpretations, and conclusions expressed in this work do not necessarily reflect the views of the World Bank, its board of executive directors, or the Iraqi government. The team retains full responsibility of data and analysis presented in this report.

Executive Summary

This Public Expenditure Review (PER) provides an integrated perspective on Iraq's need to provide better public service delivery, while maintaining macroeconomic stability and fiscal discipline. However, the achievement of these objectives unfolds within a challenging context of revenue volatility, the need to diversify the economy, pervasive corruption and weak accountability mechanisms, a rural-urban divide, and residual conflict. Reflecting these challenges, key socioeconomic developmental indicators are stalled or even declining despite rapid growth in public spending. Indeed, the review shows that growth in spending has not been matched by absorptive capacity, let alone improved outcomes.

The PER is one component of World Bank assistance to the government to improve public expenditure policy and management. Related activities are working to strengthen public financial management, promote revenue transparency (through participation in the Extractive Industries Transparency Initiative), and provide guidance on revenue management and economic diversification.

Overall, Iraq has made significant progress in macroeconomic stabilization, as large deficits and high inflation during the mid- to late-2000s have been corrected. However, the difficult task of constructing the fiscal institutions to embed the practices of good economic management remains a slow work in progress. For now, the key elements are a cautious reference oil price for the budget, a rudimentary medium-term budget strategy, and reasonable adherence to the budget law. Nonetheless, there remain extensive off-budget activities, a tendency to ad hoc midyear spending initiatives, and an absence of meaningful top-down budget ceilings.

An overarching message of the PER is that fiscal institutions are ill-equipped to deal with the complexities of an oil-dominated budget. Thus, fiscal aggregates are characterized by pronounced volatility, which is currently transmitted to spending and the broader economy, because of the absence of smoothing mechanisms. As the recent trend in oil prices has mostly been upwards, the result has been a significant ratchet effect in spending, as recurrent commitments (such as salaries) have moved up with each revenue surge. The medium-term budget strategy process has not yet proven capable of providing some restraint in this regard.

The PER's analysis of the economic classification of the budget finds, not surprisingly, that there are a few key budget drivers. Wages and compensation account for about one-third (and rising) of total spending, and nearly 40 percent of this is going to the security ministries (Interior and Defense). Underlying this is a generous wage scale put in place in 2004, various wage increases since then, and sharp growth in public sector numbers. Compounding these policy decisions are severe shortfalls in payroll management, which include major gaps in the human resources information system, and almost certainly high levels of ghost employees and double dipping.

The counterpart to the growth in public sector pay and numbers is severe administrative bloat. There are 40 ministries that make up the central government, which is at least twice the typical number. The Kurdish Regional Government (KRG) has completely mimicked the central government structure, despite the fact that it is a much smaller economy, which could easily function with a leaner level of administration.

Transfers and subsidies account for about one-fifth of total spending and have a small number of key drivers: the public distribution system (PDS), pensions, and fuel subsidies. It should be noted that implicit fuel subsidies (due to below-market pricing) are even larger than on-budget subsidies. The shortfalls in the PDS are well known, and it is worth adding that the PDS mode of operation—government purchases of imported food which are then distributed—exposes the PDS to all the failings of Iraqi government procurement and logistical capacity, which have been identified in other World Bank reports. Likewise, the pension system picks up the weaknesses of the human resources management system, since most pensioners are in the public sector. Nonetheless, a sustained program of capacity building in pension management is under way and is reaping some positive results.

Overall, the social safety net provided by the PDS, pensions, and subsidies has major gaps. Subsidies lack any meaningful targeting, are inefficient in terms of beneficiary impact relative to amount spent, and are subject to corruption and mismanagement. Regarding the PDS, the objective is to reform its operation and work towards targeting and eventual monetization. This work will be gathering pace as the new household survey results come in, providing the analytical work needed to inform the policy reform. The agenda on fuel subsidies will be very challenging, as there are few success stories in Middle East and North Africa of subsidy reform. Furthermore, continued gaps in electricity service (discussed further below) will mean a constant temptation to quick fixes (that is, to enable local generators), with further subsidies and associated vested interests.

The financing of state-owned enterprises (SOEs) is a particularly opaque section of the budget, and has direct implications for private sector development as these enterprises are crowding out private firms and impeding factor reallocation. Most of the budget funding goes towards employee wages, but whether the enterprise is active or not has to be assessed on a case-by-case basis; currently there is no SOE information system which can provide such clarity. The government has made periodic attempts to move "viable" SOEs onto bank financing, but this presumes a level of capacity that many SOEs do not have, and in any event as the banks are state owned, this does nothing to reform the broader public sector.

Regarding the capital budget, the key theme is underexecution; execution rates are currently in the 50–60 percent range. This phenomenon is getting worse over time, as the typical budgetary response to public demand for better services is to increase allocations even as capacity to spend is stalled. This is compounded by a lack of knowledge about what is happening to capital allocations at the provincial and local level, but it is clear that mismanagement and opportunities for corruption are rife. The country's dated procurement law is making things worse, because its Egyptian-style focus on multiple signatures and approvals for every transaction invites shortcuts and sidestepping that open the door for corruption. Despite the lack of absorptive capacity, the government has failed to make use of public-private partnerships or other means to leverage private sector capacity. KRG is a notable exception in this regard.

The functional classification of spending produces similar messages to the economic classification, namely administrative bloat, and heavy spending on security and market interventions. The PER shows that within each function there is an unbalanced pattern of spending towards distortions, for example on purchases of fuel, and mismanaged social protection measures.

The counterpart to high spending on security and administration is that some vital sectors are being neglected. The most important examples are health and housing, where an expectation of substantial needs, given the effect of war, meets the reality that Iraq underspends in these sectors, even compared to countries without legacies of violence and destruction. Although the reasons for this need to be explored through in-depth sector reviews, it appears that for health, the system never coped with the transition from having United Nations (UN) provision in the sanctions era to becoming solely a responsibility of the Iraqi government.

The PER then examines the strategic framework for the budget and how this gets translated into practice. Iraq does not lack strategic documents, including the National Development Plan (NDP) and the poverty reduction strategy (PRS), and there are numerous reports from external partners that provide guidance to policy makers. However, there is a major gap between rhetoric and reality in the NDP and PRS. In particular, the NDP's discussion of private sector development and decentralization bears little resemblance to the situation on the ground. Neither the NDP nor the PRS had a meaningful focus on spending efficiency, and both have been out of cycle with the budget formulation process. By the time that the pressure for supplemental budgets comes, the strategic element has evaporated.

In principle, the options for Iraq to improve the strategic content of the annual budget formulation and implementation are well known: the challenge is to determine which option best matches Iraq's needs and capacity. The (nonexclusive) options include a strengthening of the current reference oil price role in the budget, a fiscal rule, some means to limit spending volatility, and a revenue saving fund such as the transition fund proposed in the Country Economic Memorandum. However, this choice should not distract from other urgent measures that would improve fiscal management, in particular the need to limit and eventually eliminate off-budget spending. The Integrated Financial Management Information

System (IFMIS) will form an important control mechanism towards this objective.

Given the PER's focus on investment spending and the role of this spending in meeting the expectations of the public, the PER discusses how to improve public investment management. Although the entire spending cycle needs an integrated diagnostic, it is clear from the analysis provided by the PER that there are some bottlenecks that need to be tackled immediately. These include the budget treatment of capital commitments (which is essentially a botched accrual method), the processing of letters of credit (which can take up to five months), and chronic weaknesses in capacity, from feasibility studies all the way to project implementation. There are some signs of progress, especially with regard to project monitoring by the Ministry of Planning, and capacity building can address some of the downstream issues. This leaves the upstream factors as being in need of the most attention.

The PER concludes with an outline of issues facing two essential service delivery sectors: electricity and health. While both are similar in terms of mounting frustration of the public, the sector issues are quite different.

Electricity has received a high-quality strategic analysis, and the investment needs are reasonably well understood, even if implementation is sometimes frantic and disjointed. However, there are major challenges in terms of funding due to the tariff structure (which is too low and has no meaningful marginal cost pricing), bill collection shortfalls, and an outdated institutional structure. Furthermore, the government is still struggling to integrate its electricity plans with those for gas, since there would be numerous benefits to using natural gas for electricity generation.

On the other hand, the health system is in deep crisis, and even the basic framework (that is, whether to fund from general revenues or insurance) is not settled. As mentioned above, institutional arrangements in health were directly affected by the sanctions regimen, and the system was then overwhelmed by the years of violence following the overthrow of the Saddam regime in 2003. In future work, triangulation of spending flows with services received at the facility level will be essential to get a complete picture of the sector's performance.

Recommendations for future work flow from the PER's findings. Given the recurring finding that Iraq's actual budget process is increasingly untethered from strategic considerations, there is a clear up-stream agenda on the medium-term fiscal framework and its link to the annual budget cycle. Public investment management is a crosscutting capability that is needed to meet all of Iraq's sector objectives. And as discussed above, key sectors face specific challenges and circumstances that warrant an in-depth focus.

Abbreviations

BSA	Board of Supreme Audit
BSP	bulk supply point
CCGT	combined cycle gas turbine
CEM	Country Economic Memorandum
CGD	Center for Global Development
CoM	Council of Ministers
CoMSec	Council of Ministers Secretariat
CoR	Council of Representatives
CPARs	Country Procurement Assessment Reviews
DFI	Development Fund for Iraq
DG	diesel generator
DID	Department for International Development
DPL	Development Policy Loan
DPT	diphtheria
EIA	Energy Information Administration
EITI	Extractive Industries Transparency Initiative
FML	Financial Management Law
EMR	Eastern Mediterranean Region
GCC	Gulf Cooperation Council
GDF	Global Development Finance
GDP	gross domestic product
GoI	Government of Iraq
HSE	Health, Safety, and Environment
IAMB	International Advisory and Monitoring Board
ID	Iraqi dinar
IEA	International Energy Agency
IFMIS	Integrated Financial Management Information System
IG	inspector general
ILO	International Labour Organization

IMF   International Monetary Fund
INES   Integrated National Energy Strategy
INESTA   Integrated National Energy Strategy Technical Assistance
IOCs   international oil companies
IPP   independent power producer
I-PSM   Iraq Public Sector Modernization Program
KRG   Kurdish Regional Government
LC   letters of credit
LEB   life expectancy at birth
LV   low voltage
MDA   ministries, departments, and agencies
MDG   Millennium Development Goals
MENA   Middle East and North Africa
MMPW   Ministry of Municipalities and Public Works
MoB   Municipality of Baghdad
MoE   Ministry of Electricity
MoF   Ministry of Finance
MoH   Ministry of Health
MOHESR   Ministry of Higher Education and Scientific Research
MoI   Ministry of Industry
MoO   Ministry of Oil
MoP   Ministry of Planning
MoT   Ministry of Trade
MTFF   Medium-Term Fiscal Framework
NBP   National Board of Pensions
NDP   National Development Plan
NOC   North Oil Company
NPV   net present value
O&M   operations and maintenance
OECD   Organization for Economic Cooperation and Development
OOP   out-of-pocket
OPEX   operating expenses
OPRA   Oil Proceeds Revenue Account
PDS   Public Distribution System
PEFA   Public Expenditure and Financial Accountability
PEIA   Public Expenditure and Institutional Assessment
PER   Public Expenditure Review
PFM   Public Financial Management
PFMAP   Public Financial Management Action Plan

PIM	Public Investment Management
PIP	Public Investment Program
PRISTA	Pension Reform Implementation Support Technical Assistance
PPP	public-private partnership
PRS	Poverty Reduction Strategy
SBA	Stand-By Arrangement
SCGT	simple cycle gas turbine
SOC	South Oil Company
SOEs	state-owned enterprises
SOMO	State Oil Marketing Organization
SOOPGD	State Organization for Oil Products and Gas Distribution
SPF	State Pension Fund
SPM	single-point mooring
SPS	State Pension System
SSD	Pensions & Social Security Department
SSN	social safety net
T&D	transmission and distribution
TCM	trillion cubic meters
UNDP	United Nations Development Program
UNESCO	United Nations Educational, Scientific and Cultural Organization
UNESCWA	United Nations Economic and Social Commission for Western Asia
UNFPA	United Nations Population Fund
WDI	World Development Indicators
WHO	World Health Organization
WHO EMRO	World Health Organization Eastern Mediterranean Regional Office

Fiscal Year

January 1 – December 31

Currency and Equivalents

Currency unit = Iraqi dinar (ID)

As of June 2013
US$1 = ID1166.0

Introduction

The Republic of Iraq is a country emerging from conflict and facing the challenge of reconstructing core physical infrastructure and delivering public services to 34 million people. Its gross domestic product (GDP) per capita was estimated at US$6,305 in 2012,[1] putting Iraq in the category of middle-income countries. Its economy is dominated by oil: Iraq produces about 3.0 million barrels per day, and crude oil accounts for nearly half of GDP and over 90 percent of total exports. The contribution of non-oil sectors is relatively small both in GDP and in exports, and the role of the private sector in the economy is very limited.

Decades of conflict and sanctions have left the Iraqi economy, institutions, and infrastructure in tatters. While efforts are under way to repair and replace damaged infrastructure and institutions, progress is hampered by politics, lack of security, and the governance environment. There has been progress in reconstructing water supply systems, sewage treatment plants, electricity production, hospitals and health clinics, schools, housing, and transportation systems, but there remains a lot more to be done. The conflict post-2003 had a particularly severe impact on the economy: the oil export infrastructure was either damaged or vandalized; large factories, especially those connected with the military, were destroyed; and energy production plants, production laboratories, and water supply and sanitation systems were damaged. In addition, the conflict caused a significant exodus, including public sector workers, weakening public sector capacity and institutions.

Public spending, including capital investment, is necessary to repair and rehabilitate the Iraqi economy, but the government has faced challenges to prioritize and implement a capital investment program. As a resource-rich economy, Iraq has considerable resources in the form of oil receipts to finance a capital investment program. At the same time, the country also faces several challenges that arise from this situation in the form of "resource curse," "Dutch disease," and heightened tensions over who controls these resources.

A large body of literature on oil-rich economies[2] underscores several salient characteristics of these economies. A central feature is the concept of a "resource curse," the paradox that countries with an abundance of natural resources like oil tend to have less economic growth and worse development outcomes than countries with fewer natural resources. While this could happen for many different reasons, four factors are especially important:

- First, excessive dependence on oil revenues makes these countries highly vulnerable to abrupt changes in international oil prices.
- Second, a great majority of oil-rich countries fail to diversify their economies because of Dutch disease, a situation where a booming oil export industry causes rapid currency appreciation, which in turn undermines the competitiveness of other sectors, notably agriculture and manufacturing, in the world markets.
- Third, the oil funds are prone to embezzlement, corruption, and wasteful and inefficient public spending, because of weak institutions and lack of accountability. Weak institutions and accountability are in turn rooted in the fact that citizens pay little or no taxes (as oil rents finance most public spending) and less taxation of citizens implies less accountability and less public scrutiny of public spending in general.
- Finally, oil resources can, and often do, provoke conflicts within societies (Collier 2007), as different groups and factions fight for their share, and this could in turn undermine political stability and economic development.

The report is organized as follows. Chapter 1 sets out the strategic context for Iraq, including the evolving political situation, macroeconomic context, and poverty and social conditions. Chapter 2 analyzes the trends in, and composition of, public expenditure, both from economic and functional perspectives. This chapter discusses the efficiency of public expenditure in Iraq (that is, through benchmarking as well as direct output comparisons) and identifies, on the basis of analysis, key sectors for further in-depth assessment for the second phase. It also looks at revenue management issues drawing on the Country Economic Memorandum (CEM). Chapter 3 examines strategic prioritization and budget execution issues in Iraq. In particular, it reviews the national development priorities, as articulated in the National Development Plan (NDP) and poverty reduction strategy (PRS), and examines the strategic orientation of public expenditures, that is, to what extent public expenditure priorities relate to Iraq's development plan. This chapter also focuses on public investment in Iraq, analyzes key issues against efficient and effective use of investment budget, and proposes actions for an effective Public Investment Management (PIM) system. Chapter 4 analyzes efficiency of public spending in electricity sector and discusses public service delivery issues while chapter 5 focuses on efficiency and equity issues in public expenditure on health.

Notes

1. International Monetary Fund (IMF) estimates as of 2013.
2. See, for example, Sachs and Warner (1995, 2001), Gylfason et al. (1999), Leite and Weidmann (1999), Auty (2001), Moore (2007), and Lederman and Maloney (2007).

CHAPTER 1

Strategic Context

Introduction

This chapter provides a brief overview of the political, macroeconomic, and social context, and identifies the main strategic challenges that the government face. Iraq's security and political situation remain fragile, which are risks to economic growth and impediments to institutional capacity and development. Social conditions are fragile and the level of unemployment is high. Although Iraq's economic growth prospects are favorable, there are significant risks. Main risks include political factors, security issues, technical capability, and institutional capacity to implement reforms.

The Iraqi government faces the challenge of using growing oil revenues efficiently for better service delivery. Macroeconomic stability alone is not enough to address social and economic development issues and to avoid a resource curse. Iraq's oil wealth alone cannot generate sustainably high living standards for the majority of its population. Economic diversification is an imperative—both to create jobs and to promote income-generating opportunities for the Iraqi population. Key development policy challenges are (i) to use its oil wealth to promote economic diversification; and (ii) to identify and remove constraints to nonhydrocarbon economic activities. The government will need to use the revenues from oil to ensure that the country's infrastructure is reconstructed and people benefit from better social services. With the prospect of an oil boom, the government has the opportunity to take concrete steps now.

Political Developments

Iraq has suffered from a series of wars and sanctions over the last three decades. The country has had a significant security problem following the first Gulf War in 1980–88, the second Gulf War in 1991, international economic sanctions in 1991–2003, and the fall of the Saddam Hussein regime in 2003. These have left its economy, infrastructure, and institutions in tatters, and contributed to rising poverty and deteriorating social conditions.

*In March 2003, a U.S.-led invasion toppled Saddam Hussein's government,
marking the beginning of a violent conflict, with different groups competing for power.*
The conflict triggered violent crimes such as bombing attacks, armed robberies,
assassinations, and kidnappings, which, exacerbated by easy access to arms and
ammunition, wrecked havoc on the Iraqi society. Following the fall of Saddam
Hussein's regime, the United States appointed a civil administrator of Iraq, charging it with supervising Iraq's transition to democracy.

The conflict has had enormous costs in terms of casualties and loss of human lives.
Figure 1.1 shows that total documented civilian deaths since 2003 from violence
are estimated at about 123,000 people.[1] While violent attacks and the loss of
lives have dropped significantly in recent years—from their peak of about 29,000
annual deaths in 2006 to about 5,000 deaths in 2012—the country still lacks
security and stability.

Since 2003, Iraq has achieved several politically important milestones. In January
2005, some 8 million people voted in the first nationwide multiparty elections
for 50 years, electing a Transitional National Assembly. Amid escalating violence,
parliament selected as President Jalal Talabani, a Kurdish politician, former guer-
rilla leader, and cofounder of the Patriotic Union of Kurdistan. Following that,
voters approved a new constitution, which created an Islamic federal democracy.
In March 2010, more than 60 percent of Iraqis voted in a second parliamentary
election, and the former Prime Minister Iyad Allawi, head of the Iraqiya Alliance,
won the election with 91 seats, followed by Nuri Al-Maliki's State of Law
Alliance with 89 seats (out of a total of 325). With either party unable to form
a government on its own, talks began between Allawi and Maliki, and after eight
months of stalemate, parliament reelected Jalal Talabani as president, who named
Al-Maliki as prime minister.

*Following the withdrawal of U.S. troops, Iraq needs to consolidate security, stabil-
ity, and peace.* The United States completed its troop pull-out from Iraq in

Figure 1.1 Annual Documented Civilian Deaths from Violence, 2003–12

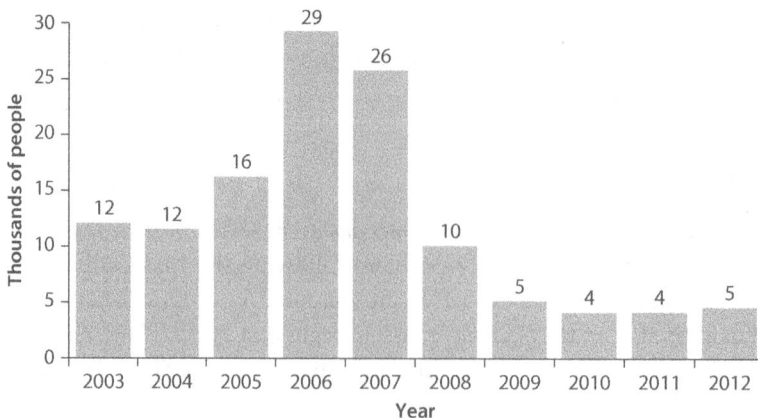

Source: Iraq Body Count (www.iraqbodycount.org).

December 2011. Unfortunately, this pull-out has been followed by an apparent disarray in the Unity Government of Iraq,[2] with political fault lines reemerging between the Shiite and Sunni groups in the government, and the Al-Iraqiya (Sunni) parliamentary bloc boycotting parliament and Cabinet sessions. The political conflict has in turn triggered a wave of bombing attacks, raising fears of escalating violence. Despite this setback, violence remains at its lowest level over the last two years.

The Macroeconomic Context

Amidst a very challenging political and security environment, Iraq has achieved considerable progress toward macroeconomic stability since 2003. It has achieved single-digit inflation, economic growth has resumed, and both fiscal balance and current account balance have improved (after having deteriorated in the wake of the global financial crisis). Iraq's debt to gross domestic product (GDP) ratio has decreased thanks to the debt restructuring with the Paris Club and other creditors. The macro stabilization program has been supported by International Monetary Fund (IMF), through its successive Stand-By Arrangements (SBA), while the Bank's Fiscal Sustainability Development Policy Loan (DPL), approved in February 2010, supported structural reforms in budget management, the social protection system, and the financial sector.

After collapsing by around 41 percent in 2003, real GDP growth rate has recovered since 2004, although growth has fluctuated significantly from year to year (figure 1.2). The fluctuation in GDP growth (boom-bust cycle) is in part tied to the performance of the oil sector: Following the 2003 conflict, oil production and exports declined. Iraq's economic performance had deteriorated significantly at the end of 2008 due to the oil price shock. More recently, due to high oil prices and increased oil production, real GDP grew by 8.4 percent in 2012. Crude oil production and exports have steadily increased in recent years, with crude oil production rising from 2 million barrels per day in 2004 to 3 million barrels per day in 2012. Similarly, oil exports have increased from 1.5 million barrels per day in 2004 to 2.4 million barrels per day in 2012. At the same time, oil prices for the Iraqi crude oil, after dipping in 2009 in the wake of the global financial crisis, have continued to increase (figure 1.5), with prices reaching US$107 per barrel in 2012. Inflation, after reaching a peak of over 50 percent in 2006, has declined since and stands at about 6.1 percent in 2012. This has been achieved through a combination of tight monetary policy, dinar appreciation, and a favorable fiscal situation supported by high oil prices.

The bulk of Iraq's fiscal revenue comes from oil receipts. During 2005–12, oil receipts accounted on average for 80.4 percent of total revenues, while taxes accounted for only about 2 percent of revenue (figure 1.6). Iraq's fiscal position is highly correlated with oil price levels. After holding a fiscal deficit of 20.5 percent of GDP in 2009 as a result of lower international oil prices, Iraq moved to a fiscal surplus of 4.1 percent of GDP in 2012 due to higher-than-budgeted oil revenues and an underexecution of the capital budget.

Republic of Iraq Public Expenditure Review • http://dx.doi.org/10.1596/978-1-4648-0294-2

Figure 1.2 GDP Growth Rate, 1998–2012

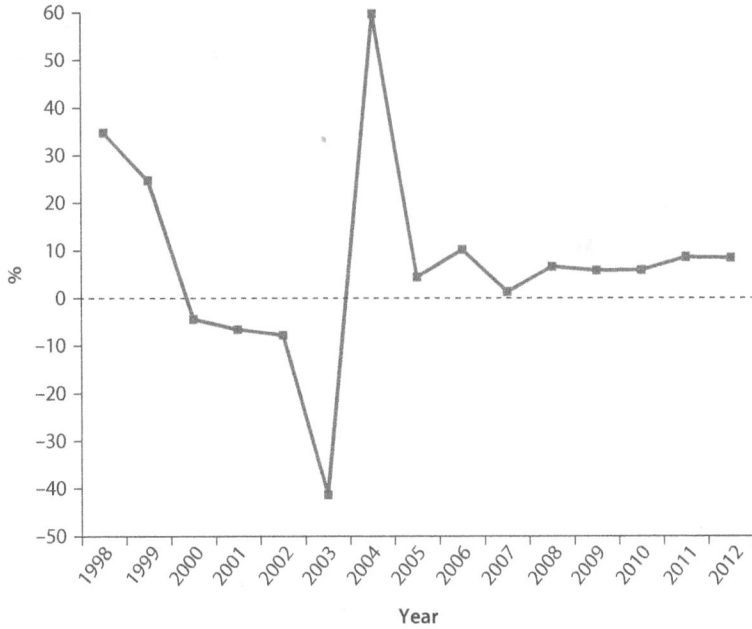

Figure 1.3 Inflation Rate, 2005–12

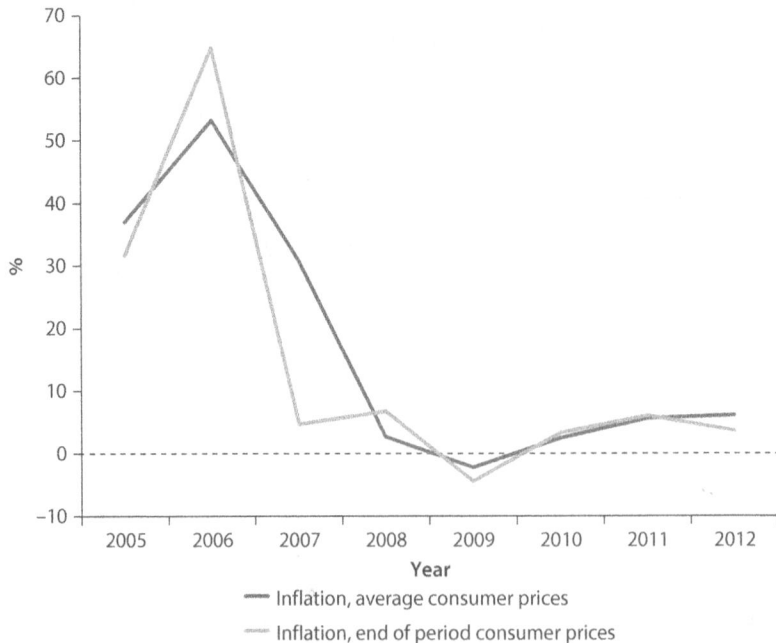

Figure 1.4 Oil Production and Exports Recovery, 2006–12

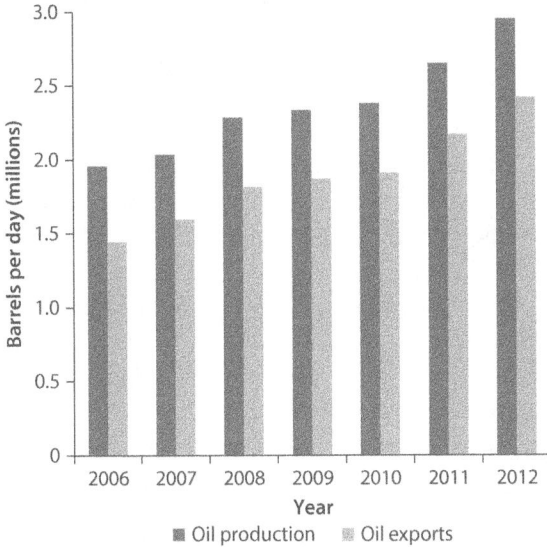

Source: IMF World Economic Outlook, October 2013.

Figure 1.5 Oil Prices Before and After Financial Crisis, 2006–12

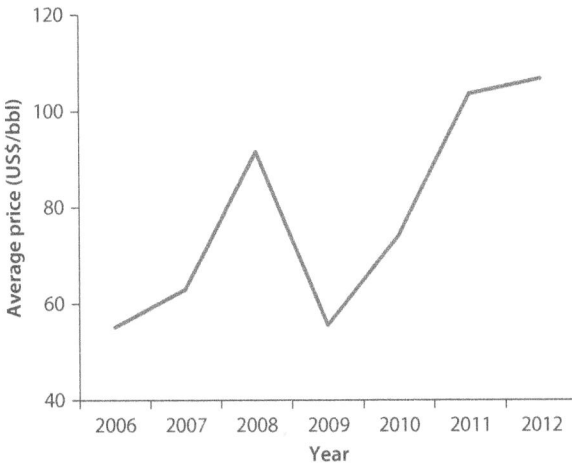

Iraq's public debt has steadily declined between 2005 and 2012 (figure 1.8), largely due to debt relief and restructuring by the Paris Club. The external debt comprises four categories: (i) Paris Club bilateral debt (33 percent of total); (ii) non-Paris Club bilateral debt (52 percent); (iii) commercial debt (15 percent); and (iv) multilateral debt (0.4 percent). In November 2004, the Paris

Club countries agreed to reduce the country's debts by 80 percent in three phases provided Iraq met a specific set of conditions. By 2007, Iraq's total external debt was reduced by 53 percent, as Iraq was able to abide by all of the conditions. Overall, Iraq's Paris Club debt fell by 68 percent between 2004 and 2007, non-Paris Club debt fell by 83 percent, and commercial debts fell by 82 percent. The successful conclusion of a Stand-By Arrangement with the IMF triggered the release of the final tranche of debt relief agreed with the Paris Club. At the same time, the authorities were able to reduce internal debt by about 30 percent over the same period, further reducing the public debt to GDP ratio of Iraq.

After staying in deficit in 2009, the current account balance has improved, with a surplus of 7 percent of GDP in 2012. The recovery in international oil prices improved the trade and current account balances substantially (figure 1.9). The current account balance remained positive in 2013.

Gross international reserves have continued to accumulate. Following significant losses between 2008 and 2009, Central Bank of Iraq's gross international reserves increased from US$50.6 billion at the end of 2010 to US$70.3 billion at the end of 2012. In the context of increasing oil prices and production, Iraq's reserves are estimated to increase to above US$77 billion by 2013. Reserve coverage in months of imports of goods and services was at 9.3 in 2012.

Figure 1.6 Sources of Total Revenues, Average, 2005–12

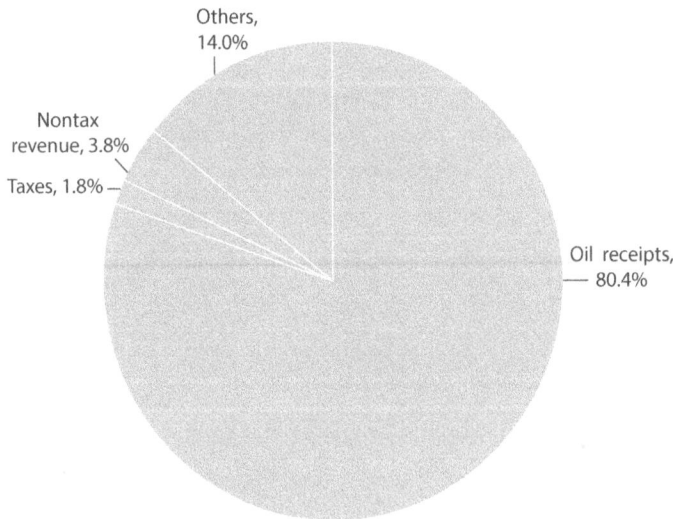

Figure 1.7 Government Spending, 2005–12

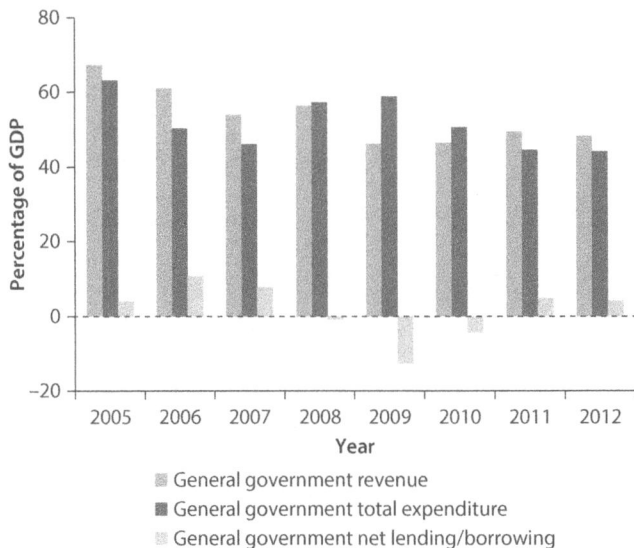

- General government revenue
- General government total expenditure
- General government net lending/borrowing

Figure 1.8 Gross Public Debt, 2005–12

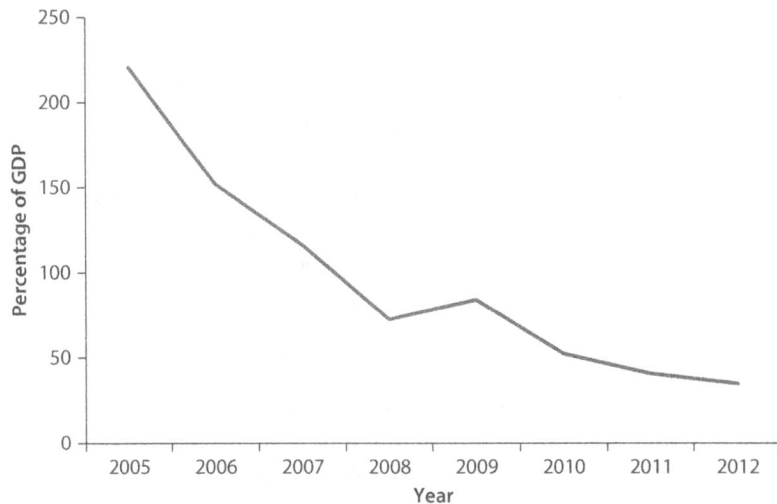

Source: IMF World Economic Outlook, October 2013.

Poverty and Social Conditions

The sanctions and conflicts have led to increased poverty and vulnerability.
According to the 2012 Household Survey, Iraq's poverty headcount index at
national poverty line is estimated at 19.8 percent in 2012. Table 1.1 presents
poverty and social indicators.[3]

Figure 1.9 Current Account Balance, 2005–12

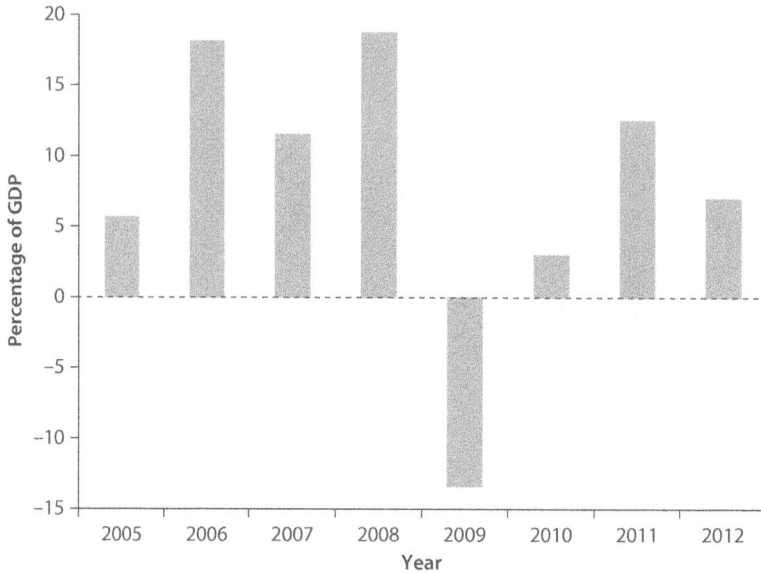

Unemployment has persisted at the rate of about 18 percent overall, with a disproportionately high rate among youths at 30 percent and among women at 32.5 percent. Among those who are employed, about 58 percent were employed in services, 23 percent in agriculture, and 18 percent in industry. The oil sector dominates GDP generation, but makes very little contribution to employment, most of which is in the public sector and agriculture.

Net primary education enrollment reached a peak of 92 percent in 2007, from 91 percent in 2005. This shows only a marginal improvement over the 87.4 percent level achieved in 2000. Primary school completion rate shows a declining trend: it declined from 78.6 percent in 2005 to 66.3 percent in 2007. The exception seems to be net secondary school enrollment, which has improved from about 32 percent in 2000 to about 45 percent in 2007.

Life expectancy at birth and child immunization coverage have fallen. Life expectancy has declined from 70.7 years in 2000 to 68 years in 2011; and immunization coverage has fallen from 78 percent in 2000 to 69 percent in 2012. Under-five mortality has improved from about 43 per thousand in 2000 to 31 per thousand in 2012, although this level is still quite high (and close to the rates in the Middle East and North Africa region's poorest countries such as Djibouti and the Republic of Yemen).

There are large disparities between the rural and urban areas in Iraq, in terms of both poverty incidence and access to social services (figure 1.10). Rural poverty incidence is more than twice the rate of poverty incidence in urban areas; and there is a significant gap between the rural and urban areas in terms of population with access to improved water sources and sanitation facilities. Beyond the urban-rural disparities, there are significant spatial disparities among the

Table 1.1 Poverty and Social Indicators, 2000, 2005, and Latest Data

	2000	2005	Latest data[a]
Poverty			
Poverty headcount ratio at $1.25 a day (PPP) (% of population)[b]	...	...	<2
Poverty headcount ratio at $2 a day (PPP) (% of population)[b]	...	...	8
Poverty headcount ratio at national poverty line (% of population)	...	...	19.8
Poverty headcount ratio at rural poverty line (% of rural population)	...	...	30.6
Poverty headcount ratio at urban poverty line (% of urban population)	...	...	14.8
Employment/Unemployment			
Employment in agriculture (% of total employment)	...	29.7	23.4
Employment in industry (% of total employment)	...	17.7	18.2
Employment in services (% of total employment)	...	52.5	58.3
Unemployment, total (% of total labor force)	...	18	17.5
Internally displaced persons (number, high estimate)	700,000	1,300,000	2,764,000
Education			
Primary completion rate, total (% of relevant age group)	55.6	78.6	66.3
School enrollment, primary (% gross)	95.4	102.1	107.5
School enrollment, primary (% net)	87.4	90.9	91.8
School enrollment, secondary (% gross)	37.5	47.7	53.1
School enrollment, secondary (% net)	32.3	40.4	44.5
Health			
Life expectancy at birth, total (years)	70.7	68.5	68
Births attended by skilled health staff (% of total)	72.1	88.5	79.7
Mortality rate, under-5 (per 1,000)	42.8	40.7	31
Maternal mortality ratio (modeled estimate, per 100,000 live births)	84	82	63
Immunization, diphteria (% of children ages 12–23 months)	78	65	69
Improved sanitation facilities (% of population with access)	69	71	73
Improved sanitation facilities, rural (% of rural population with access)	54	61	79.8
Improved sanitation facilities, urban (% of urban population with access)	76	76	86
Improved water source (% of population with access)	80	80	79
Improved water source, rural (% of rural population with access)	49	53	66.9
Improved water source, urban (% of urban population with access)	95	93	94

Source: World Bank, World Development Indicators (WDI), 2013.
Note: PPP = public-private partnership.
a. Latest data refer to the following years: health (2011); education (2007); poverty (2012); and employment/unemployment (2008).
b. Preliminary results of the 2012 Household Survey.

Figure 1.10 Poverty Incidence and Access to Social Services in Urban and Rural Areas, 2012

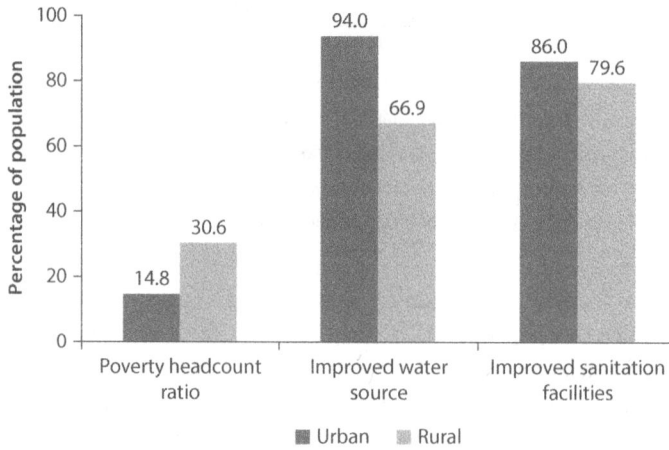

Source: World Bank, World Development Indicators, 2013.

governorates of Iraq, with higher level of deprivation and poverty in most southern and middle provinces (with the exception of Basra) and the Kurdish Regional Government (KRG).

Prospects

With the impending oil boom, Iraq's oil production and export revenues are projected to increase in the short and medium term. Real GDP growth went up by 8.4 percent in 2012 due to increased oil production and global oil prices, and is estimated to grow by 3.7 percent in 2013 due to slowdown in oil production and attacks on export infrastructure. The volume of oil exports increased by 18.2 percent in 2012, averaging 2.4 million barrels per day (mbpd). In December 2012, production was reported as exceeding 3 mbpd for the first time since 1980. Part of the increase resulted from the new single-point mooring (SPM) facility that opened in March 2012.[4] Oil production is projected to reach 3.0 mbpd in 2013 and 3.9 mbpd in 2016.

The government is seeking to boost oil output through a series of development contracts awarded to international oil companies. Its long-term goal is to lift output to an ambitious 12 mbpd. Despite the absence of a federal hydrocarbons law, the involvement of international oil companies (IOCs) in the oil sector is expected to rise significantly over the coming years. Elsewhere, exploration and production in the KRG-administered area will be stepped up. In late March 2012, Iraq announced that it had signed a preliminary agreement with a UK-based oil company to more than double output at the northern oil field of Kirkuk, possibly adding 300,000 barrels per day to Iraq's production. Besides oil, three gas fields were recently auctioned off to capture gas from oilfields in the south of the country (Economist Intelligence Unit, Iraq Country Report, April 2012).

Iraq's external position is expected to improve due to increased oil production and high international oil prices. The recovery in international oil prices improved Iraq's trade and current account balances substantially. Iraq's trade balance has been positive since 2010. Average oil export prices for Basrah and Kirkuk crude have risen steadily since June 2010 (US$71.1 per barrel) through December 2012 (US$104 per barrel). Average oil prices continued to rise and reached US$108 per barrel by February 2013. Despite limited production capacity, price increases drove up revenues by more than 60 percent between 2010 and 2012. The current account moved from a deficit of 8.3 percent of GDP in 2009 to a surplus of 7.0 percent of GDP in 2012. The current account balance is projected to remain positive during the medium term.

Strategic Challenge

The challenge for the Iraqi authorities in the years ahead will be to turn an impending oil boom into sustained welfare improvements. Amidst a very difficult security and political environment, Iraq has on the one hand shown considerable progress in terms of achieving macroeconomic stability; on the other hand, living standards have declined. Clearly, macroeconomic stability alone is not enough to address the poverty and social conditions and to foster continued prosperity of the Iraqi people. In the years to come, oil exports are set to increase from 2.5 mbpd in 2013 to approximately 3 mbpd in 2015; and oil prices are projected to increase.[5] Combined, these developments will likely generate enormous oil revenue for the economy. From a macro policy perspective, the key challenge for the authorities will therefore be how to ensure the efficient use of this growing revenue, and how to restrain the growth of current spending (in particular wage bill) to free up resources for investment in health, education, infrastructure, and regional development, while limiting the size of the budget deficit and maintaining essential safety nets and social support for the poor and disadvantaged.

The government has the opportunity to take concrete steps now. As the country emerges out of conflict and strife, and contemplates the prospect of an oil boom, its government has the opportunity to lay the foundations of a broadly diversified economy, with a reasonable footprint that provides decent public services and security while facilitating adequate economic freedom. A fundamental challenge will be to ensure that the vast oil resources are used judiciously and for the benefit of the people.

The literature on oil-rich economies[6] documents several salient features. A central feature of such economies is that they suffer from what is known as the "resource curse," the paradox that countries with an abundance of natural resources like oil tend to have less economic growth and worse development outcomes than countries with fewer natural resources. These could happen for many different reasons, but four key factors are: volatility of revenue, lack of economic diversification, wasteful spending and weak institutions and accountability, and conflicts or civil war.

- **Volatility of revenues:** When government revenues are dominated by inflows from natural resources such as oil, international oil price swings can wreck havoc with government planning. Revenue volatility, in the absence of stabilization mechanisms, translates into spending volatility, fluctuations in budget deficit, and/or government's overdependence on domestic financing. The capacity to handle short-term fluctuations in revenues and keeping them in line with spending is thus critical. In addition, while Iraq faces a longer-term depletion horizon than most other oil producers, excessively rapid resource depletion, with insufficient savings for future generations, is also a concern.
- **Lack of diversification:** A great majority of oil-rich developing countries fail to diversify their economies because of "Dutch disease," a phenomenon where a booming oil export industry causes rapid currency appreciation, undermining other productive sectors' competitiveness, notably agriculture and manufacturing, in the world markets. The increasing national oil revenue often results in higher government spending that increases the real exchange rate and raises wages, crowding out other tradable sectors.
- **Wasteful spending and weak institutions and accountability:** Huge flows of money from oil resources can fuel wasteful and inefficient spending, patronage, and political corruption. In economies that are not resource dependent, governments tax citizens, who in return demand efficient and responsive government. This bargain establishes a political accountability between government and citizens. In oil-rich economies, however, citizens pay little or no taxes (as all revenues come from oil rents) which means there exists little or no incentives for scrutiny of public spending and service delivery. At the same time, politicians often find it easier to maintain authority through allocating the oil rents to favored constituents rather than through putting in place growth-oriented economic policies and fiscal institutions, including taxation. The result is a vicious circle of lack of political accountability: less taxation implies less public scrutiny of spending and low efficiency and poor service delivery, which further limits the opportunities for citizen taxation and participation (see McGuirk for a study of this cycle).[7]
- **Conflicts:** Oil resources can, and often do, provoke conflicts (Collier 2007), as different groups and factions fight for their share. Conflicts can occur over the control and exploitation of resources and the allocation of their revenues. Sometimes they emerge openly as separatist conflicts in regions where the resources are produced but often the conflicts occur in more hidden forms, such as fights over budgetary allocations. This tends to erode the governments' legitimacy and ability to function effectively.

A first step toward meeting these challenges would be to ensure transparency of oil revenue as well as how that revenue is used. Here, Iraq has recently taken a positive step toward greater oil revenue transparency. As part of its commitment under the Extractive Industries Transparency Initiative (EITI), the global standard for transparency of resource revenues, the Government of Iraq committed in 2008 to publish all revenues from oil sector. In December 2011, it has made progress on that commitment: the government has published the first Iraq EITI Report,[8] which details production figures and revenues from the sales of oil abroad in 2009. The report shows that Iraq received about US$41 billion in revenue from oil and gas exports in 2009. A comparison and reconciliation of the oil sector production and exports found that there was a discrepancy of about a US$1 billion out of a total oil revenue of about US$41 billion, with the discrepancies all explained by "timing differences, or as being the result of items initially omitted in certain parties' reporting." In the future, the EITI reports plan to include signature bonuses and noncash oil exports as well as revenues from the mining sector. While there is clearly a need to speed up the publication of EITI reports, there is no doubt that this first step provides a good basis upon which further meaningful analyses of public spending efficiency and effectiveness can be undertaken.[9]

However, oil revenue transparency alone is not enough. The authorities will need to put in place additional steps. First, a mechanism for effective revenue management must be put in place, both in terms of fiscal stabilization and reducing the impact of global oil price swings on revenue and expenditure, and also in terms of ensuring that any potential concerns of a mismatch between resource depletion and insufficient savings for future generations are addressed. Second, the authorities will need to diversify the economy away from oil into other sectors, an issue that is addressed in the Iraq Country Economic Memorandum, prepared concurrently with this report. Third, regardless of the revenue management mechanism eventually put in place, the authorities will need to enhance the strategic orientation and efficiency of public expenditure. This is discussed in chapters 2 and 3. Finally, the authorities will need to create mechanisms to break the vicious circle of lack of accountability, the root cause of wasteful spending and weak institutions. This is the toughest challenge for the authorities, but there is much that Iraq can learn from other resource-rich countries that have been successful in avoiding a resource curse.

Notes

1. See Iraq Body Count (www.iraqbodycount.org); the estimates are as of December, 2012.

2. The Al-Maliki government issued an arrest warrant against Sunni Vice President Tareq Al-Hashemi, charging that he ran operations that targeted Shiite officials. Al-Hashemi has denied the charges, left the country, and refused to return for trial in Baghdad. In protest, his party, the Al-Iraqiya parliamentary bloc, has boycotted parliament.

3. Analytical work on Iraq faces significant data constraints. Long time series and comparable data are hard to obtain. Due to a paucity of surveys and capacity constraints, most socioeconomic and human development indicators are either not available or are not up to date. The lack of regular and up to date data limits the ability to reliably assess the country's progress over time, especially in areas such as poverty and social conditions.

4. The SPM has a nameplate capacity of 850,000 b/d but will only increase exports by 400,000 b/d for the coming year and is expected to reach full capacity only by end-

2013. This SPM is the first of five planned offshore loading buoys to be installed by 2014. Iraq's production capacity has exceeded its export capabilities since mid-2011, and the completion of the new SPM, which will only operate at half of nameplate capacity this year, brings some much needed relief to this particular bottleneck (Economist Intelligence Unit, Iraq Country Report, April 2012).

5. Oil export and revenue projections are from the IMF World Economic Outlook database.

6. See Sachs and Warner (1995, 2001), Gylfason et al. (1999), Leite and Weidmann (1999), Auty (2001), Moore (2007), and Lederman and Maloney (2007).

7. In an effort to combat resource revenue corruption, several recent reports advocate direct distribution of revenues. Under this proposal, a government would transfer some or all of the revenue from natural resource extraction to citizens in a universal, transparent, and regular payment. Devarajan et al. (2010) (Shantayanan Devarajan, Tuan Minh Le, and Gaël Raballand, "Increasing Public Expenditure Efficiency in Oil-rich Economies: A Proposal," World Bank Policy Research Working Paper #5287, April) and the Center for Global Development's Oil to Cash Paper series ("Oil-to-Cash: Fighting the Resource Curse through Cash Transfers") are examples of such recent reports. For a specific report about Iraq, see "Iraq's Last Window: Diffusing the Risks of a Petro-State," Center for Global Development (CGD) Working Paper 266 by Johnny West, September 2011.

8. The first Iraq EITI report is entitled "Iraqi Extractive Industries Transparency Initiative (IEITI): Reconciliation of Cash Inflows from the Petroleum Industry in Iraq in 2009," December 2011, and can be found at the IEITI website at http://ieiti.org.iq/ArticleShow.aspx?ID=36.

9. Iraq is now embarking on its second reconciliation for the year 2010, which will cover all revenues from oil produced and exported, but also those from active "Service Contracts" and new "Production Sharing Contracts" signed since 2009, including in KRG. The next reconciliation will still focus on revenues from oil exports, and encompass those from the ongoing exploration and development activities, including KRG and covering signature bonuses, rent and taxes. It will also aim to acquire a better grasp of domestic market consumption, to reconcile all revenues derived from oil and gas production, and include revenue from other minerals (World Bank Back-to-Office Report: EITI Mission to Iraq, March 2012).

CHAPTER 2

Redirecting Government Expenditure

Introduction

Following on from the political, macro-fiscal, and social context provided in the previous chapter, this chapter reviews three key areas of fiscal policy: (i) the size of the government; (ii) revenues and main revenue management issues; and (iii) public spending issues by economic and functional classification. The analysis focuses on key expenditure policy issues, including cyclicality of government spending, public employment and wages, social expenditures, and capital spending.

Iraq is facing a number of fundamental challenges related to the level and distribution of its public spending, and to address these issues the Iraqi government has recently embarked upon several important reform initiatives in key areas of expenditure. If successfully executed, reforms in areas such as subsidies and safety nets, employment in state-owned enterprises (SOEs), and size and composition of the civil service will contribute to a higher degree of efficiency in public spending. This chapter identifies that the challenges related to general government expenditure are multifold and do not only include the currently very large spending on defense and security. As Iraq gains stability and security over time, opportunities may exist for reorientation of spending toward capital investment or social services, to provide better service delivery to the Iraqi population.

Key findings include the following:

- The state has been allowed to grow to a size that is unusually large by any standard, yet access to even basic services is deficient. This is because much of the spending goes to the core machinery of the state (general administration and security), wages and subsidies, crowding out funding for services to the population and the reconstruction of infrastructure.
- Public spending ratchets up each time oil revenues go up. There are bottlenecks in public investment, and budget execution rate is low at around 50–60 percent of overall capital budget allocation. Although capital budget allocations have increased in recent years, Iraq's ability to follow through on investment programs has been low.

- Iraq's wage bill is very high, and is the most rapidly growing budget item. Higher oil revenues translate into higher wage bill. Payroll and HR practices are weak—significant resources are being wasted through inappropriate practices.
- Social benefits, pensions, and subsidies together constitute a high share in the budget, which are highly inefficient and ineffective. In addition, the SOEs receive large subsidies from the budget, and there are also other off-budget forms of SOE finances.

The Size of the Government

The public sector in Iraq is large in proportion to the economy by any standard. The size of the public sector, measured by public-spending-to-gross domestic product (GDP) ratio, is one of the highest in the region, even though it is volatile (due to the volatility of GDP).[1] According to the International Monetary Fund (IMF) data, between 2005 and 2012, total general government expenditure averaged 52 percent of GDP. While the high spending to some extent reflects postwar reconstruction and public investment in the state-owned oil sector, it is nevertheless still large in comparison to other economies: The regional average for public expenditure to GDP in Middle East and North Africa has been about 30 percent over the same period (figure 2.1); 41 percent in advanced economies; and 29 percent in other emerging and developing economies.

The public sector in Iraq is the largest employer. Staffing of the public sector is estimated at approximately 2.8 million, with just over 2 million employed as civilians (including some 623,000 teachers), approximately 263,000 in the armed forces, and at least 500,000 working in state-owned enterprises. While

Figure 2.1 General Government Total Expenditure, 2005–12

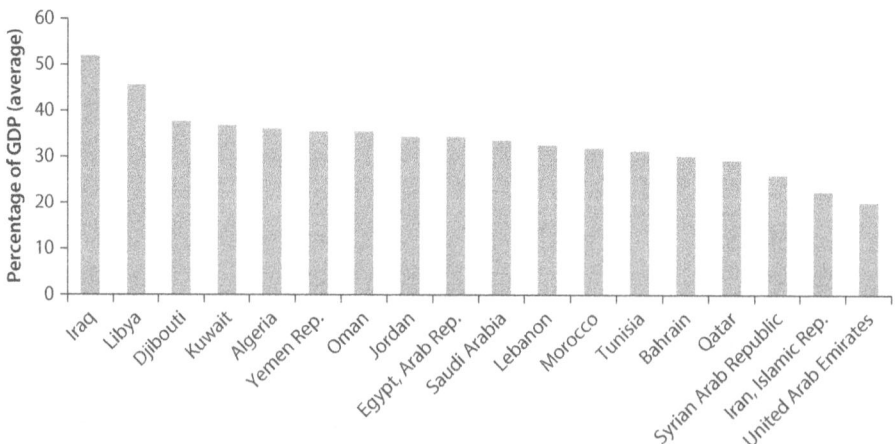

Source: IMF, World Economic Outlook, October 2013.

further work is needed to establish the exact number of public sector employees, including SOEs, by establishment, pay, and grading structure, and geographical location at the central, regional, governorate, and district levels, it is clear that reducing the size of government will require restructuring of the public sector, as well as creating the conditions for the private sector to provide more employment opportunities.

Government Revenues and Main Revenue Management Issues

Oil is by far the largest source of revenues. Iraq's revenues (including tax and non-tax revenues and grants) have increased from ID 55.1 trillion in 2009 to ID 119.4 trillion in 2012. Oil revenues had the highest increase in total, averaging 80.4 percent of overall revenues between 2005 and 2012. Oil revenues accounted for 93 percent of total revenues and 42.1 percent of GDP in 2013. On the other hand, tax revenues have been growing slowly, increasing from 1.2 percent of GDP in 2005 to 2.4 percent of GDP in 2011.

Revenues from oil flow into the Development Fund for Iraq (DFI). Oil is marketed by State Oil Marketing Organization (SOMO), which sets the price of oil—loosely based on the Saudi price. Once the letter of credit from the buyers who negotiate a sale reaches the Trade Bank of Iraq, SOMO instructs the oil producing companies, North Oil Company (NOC) and South Oil Company (SOC), to proceed with the sale, that is, ship or load the oil into pipelines to be exported. NOC's oil is mainly sent through the pipeline in the north, whereas SOC mostly ships oil through the Basra terminal. All revenues go into the Oil Proceeds Revenue Account (OPRA), 5 percent of the proceeds go as reparations payments to Kuwait, and the remaining 95 percent go into the DFI. The Iraqi Financial Management Law contains provisions on accountability and audit oversight, including publication of financial reports of oil revenues.[2] Implementation of this law is important to have better accountability and audit oversight. Control and audit are key pillars in the accountability process and deserve high attention from the Government of Iraq (GoI) and donors.[3]

The heavy dependence on oil has two key implications for fiscal policy and institutions: first, it subjects revenue and therefore expenditure to volatility of international oil prices. Second, the dependence of government on oil receipts (and the negligible contribution of tax revenues) to fund the budget means that the authorities face little or no incentive to build strong budgetary institutions and transparency, encouraging instead a top-down fiscal policy where public scrutiny of expenditure and accountability is weak. Indeed, the latter is a central challenge of fiscal policy in Iraq.

Iraq's extreme dependence on crude oil exports makes it challenging to conduct fiscal policy with a medium-term orientation. Oil export revenues are highly vulnerable to volatile international oil prices. Iraq has been subject to major fluctuations in its oil revenues. For example, after peaking at US$92 a barrel in 2008, oil prices plunged by US$56 a barrel in 2009, before starting a gradual recovery and reaching an average of US$107 in 2012. The impact on Iraq's total

Table 2.1 Budget: Revenues, 2005–12

ID billion

	2005 Original Budget	2005 Actuals	2006 Original Budget	2006 Actuals	2007 Original Budget	2007 Actuals (BSA)	2008 Original Budget	2008 Actuals (BSA)	2009 Original Budget	2009 Actuals (MOF)	2010 Original Budget	2010 Actuals (MOF)	2011 Original Budget	2011 Estimated Actuals	2012 Original Budget
Revenue	**28,850**	**40,436**	**45,392**	**49,056**	**42,056**	**54,956**	**80,476**	**80,641**	**50,409**	**55,140**	**61,735**	**70,178**	**80,935**	**99,999**	**102,327**
Oil Receipts	27,874	39,454	42,288	46,908	39,092	51,599	72,893	77,377	43,070	48,872	56,050	60,131	71,873	90,189	94,378
Taxes	622	492	2,417	594	909	1,763	1,023	2,917	3,488	1,541	1,168	1,248	2,269	1,620	2,480
Direct Taxes	219	201	1,615	354	—	—	559	—	970	1,006	600	699	653	788	1,185
Payable by Individuals	219	201	1,615	354	—	—	193	—	290	312	200	315	203	159	464
Payable by Corporations and Other enterprises	—	—	—	—	—	—	270	—	390	579	200	277	250	340	305
Companies Tax (Oil Companies)	—	—	—	—	—	—	—	—	—	—	—	—	—	—	300
Taxes on Payroll and Workforce	—	—	—	—	—	—	96	—	290	115	200	107	200	289	116
Indirect Taxes	403	291	802	240	—	—	464	—	2,518	535	568	549	1,616	832	1,295
Reconstruction tax	—	—	634	—	—	—	404	—	508	482	508	507	1,316	700	965
Exise on Petroleum Derivatives	—	—	168	—	423	349	60	—	2,010	53	60	42	300	132	330
Interest	—	—	—	—	423	353	402	—	838	134	432	45	200	48	50
Treasury Share from General companies' Profits	355	190	223	1,219	1,154	317	1,570	—	2,918	1,496	2,000	3,463	2,500	4,973	2,591
Other Nontax Revenues	—	300	465	335	462	1,207	4,588	—	95	3,097	2,085	5,291	4,093	3,169	2,828
Social Contributions	—	—	—	—	8	17	—	236	—	—	—	—	—	—	—
Grants	—	—	—	—	1	15	—	55	—	—	—	—	—	—	—
Sale of non-Financial Assets (Investments)	—	—	—	—	7	7	—	56	—	—	—	—	—	—	—

Source: Medium–Term Fiscal Framework (MTFF), 2013–15.

Note: BSA = Board of Supreme Audit; MOF = Ministry of Finance; — = not available.

revenues—and thus on its economy—was devastating. Iraq's fiscal balance worsened from a deficit of 1.3 percent of GDP in 2008 to a deficit of 20.5 percent of GDP in 2009. Real GDP declined due to the slump in international oil prices and stagnating petroleum output.

Spending is procyclical and ratchets up with each oil price surge. Government spending decisions are highly correlated to revenue trends. Figure 2.2 shows that changes in expenditure patterns have tended to follow revenue levels.

Iraq's fiscal policy framework needs to be reoriented in order to mitigate oil dependence and oil price vulnerability, as well as to foster economic diversification. A range of short-term and longer-term fiscal policy tools can be combined to manage volatility, uncertainty, and exhaustibility of oil revenue, including origination from abroad (through exports). This includes:

- Delinking government expenditures from short-term oil revenues
- Safeguarding expenditure quality through stronger public financial management (PFM) mechanisms
- Applying long-term fiscal sustainability benchmarks to public spending levels
- Continuing to implement the Medium-Term Fiscal Framework (MTFF).

The Bank is assisting Iraq in this endeavor both through a Country Economic Memorandum on "Oil Revenue Management for Economic Diversification" and through the Public Expenditure Review. Between the Country Economic Memorandum (CEM) and the Public Expenditure Review (PER), the Bank is helping Iraq with an analytical framework to make informed decisions on the

Figure 2.2 Revenues and Expenditures, 2008–12

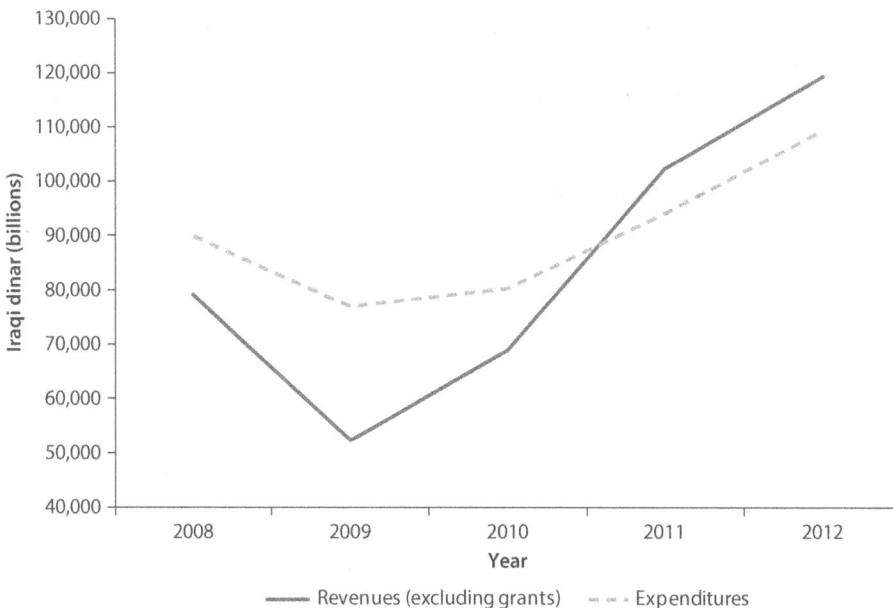

Source: IMF, World Economic Outlook, 2013.

Republic of Iraq Public Expenditure Review • http://dx.doi.org/10.1596/978-1-4648-0294-2

short- and long-term allocation of its overall resource envelope, which is domi-nated by oil revenues. The CEM aims to help develop a macro-fiscal framework to assist Iraqi policy makers in measuring petroleum financial flows and making informed spending and saving decisions consistent with the government's eco-nomic vision. The PER is focusing on spending and investment links within the overall framework described in figure 2.3.

The PER is complemented by analysis being undertaken in parallel as part of the CEM. The first stage of the CEM is focused on revenue management and eco-nomic diversification. The revenue management component has considerable overlap with the PER and informs two questions in particular, namely the appro-priate spending composition for Iraq and the role of overseas savings in the over-all fiscal strategy.

Regarding the composition of spending, the CEM finds that Iraq's economic con-ditions would warrant spending much of the additional oil revenue over the next few years on domestic capital. This is because the developmental needs of the econo-my are significant and the return on capital is very high. However, this is offset in the near term by the deficiencies in public investment management (see chapter 3 of this PER). Benchmarked from other countries, there is a risk that up to 50 percent of capital spending allocations could be dissipated in investment management shortcomings.

This leads to the second question posed, regarding overseas saving. The CEM recommends that Iraq should consider a sovereign "parking" fund, as opposed to a wealth fund, where oil revenues would be housed until spending efficiency improves. Over time, revenues in the fund would be allocated to domestic spending, where their return would be higher as the challenges identified in the PER are addressed. The CEM has developed a simple analytical model that will allow the government to conduct a range of scenarios for the spending-saving trade-off.

The CEM finds that although this strategy leads to somewhat lower consumption in the near term, it results in much higher domestic capital and foreign assets—and therefore higher sustainable consumption—in the medium term. Other means to

Figure 2.3 Managing Oil Revenues

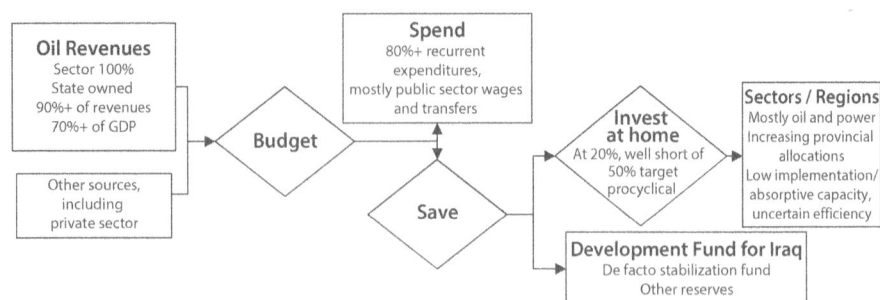

Source: Concept Note on "Iraq Programmatic Country Economic Memorandum: Managing Oil Revenues," World Bank, January 2011.

improve household welfare, such as service delivery effectiveness and trade logistics (which lower the effective price of consumption goods) can deliver near-term gains to households while the revenue management strategy is being implemented.

General Government Expenditure

This section reviews and analyzes aggregate trends in public spending and the evolution of the composition of government spending and revenues over the period 2005–11. The evolution of budget composition is analyzed by economic and functional classifications to identify major trends and key issues. The level and composition of public expenditure planned and executed by recurrent and capital breakdowns are presented. In addition, public spending by administrative classification, including Kurdish Regional Government (KRG), is presented in appendix B.

Economic Composition of Government Expenditure

One of the key objectives of the proposed approach would be to curb the escalation of current spending. Between 2005 and 2010, the Government of Iraq on average spent about 82 percent of its expenditure on recurrent expenditure, 17 percent on capital expenditure, and 1 percent on net acquisition of nonfinancial assets.[4] Trends and economic composition of government expenditure are presented in table 2.4. A closer look at the recurrent expenditure shows that employees compensation (or wages and salaries) is by far the single largest item (figure 2.4), accounting on average for over 30 percent of total expenditure, followed by purchases of goods and services (14 percent); social benefits (12 percent); pensions and grants (5 percent each); and subsidies (4 percent).

Wage Bill

Iraq's wage bill, at an average of 30 percent of total expenditure or 18 percent of GDP during 2005–10, is extraordinarily high. The government wage bill is not only a major component of recurrent spending, but it has also been the most rapidly growing item since 2005. From 2005 to 2010, the share of wage bill in the budget increased from 30 percent to 47 percent of the Iraqi public expenditure. Furthermore, evidence points to the fact that higher national oil revenue results in higher wage bills a percentage of GDP (figure 2.5), with wage adjustments lagging behind revenue changes. Appendix C shows that the Ministry of Interior is getting the highest share of compensation of employees from the budget (25.6 percent of total compensation allocations in the 2012 budget) followed by the Ministry of Education (21 percent), Ministry of Defense (11.7 percent), and Ministry of Health (8 percent). Better control of the growth of the wage bill is clearly a key area, and will provide opportunities for reorienting public spending toward capital investment and/or social services.

Iraq's wage bill is high, even by regional standards. From 2005 to 2010, the share of compensation of employees in GDP increased from 12 percent to 25

Figure 2.4 Economic Composition of Public Expenditure, Average, 2005–10

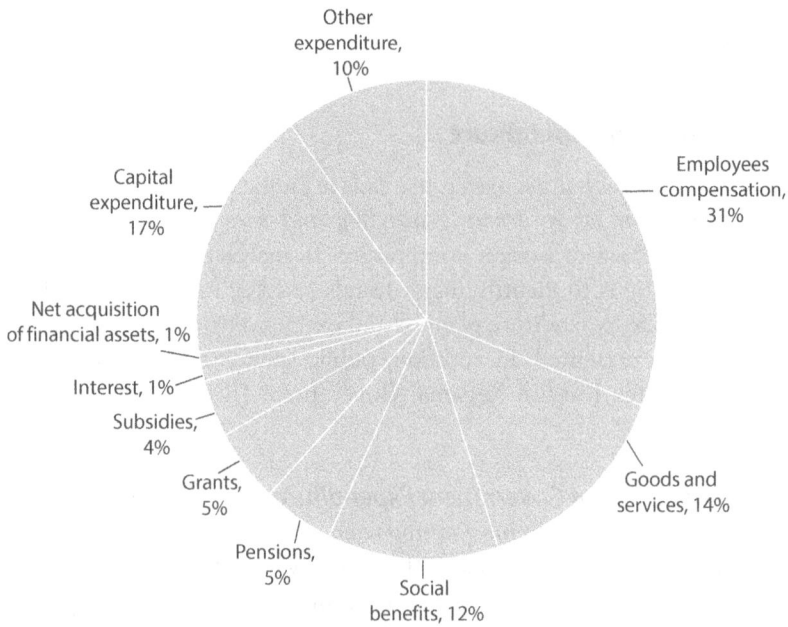

Source: Medium-Term Fiscal Framework (MTFF), 2013–15.
Note: Goods and services: All expenses on commodity and service requirements, assets maintenance, and allocations for goods and services consumed by government departments. Social benefits: Allocations for Public Distribution System (PDS; ration card), social protection network, allowances of military employees, and expenses for relief and aid for refugees. Grants: Allocations of abroad and international commitments, and grants given to service/cultural/media organizations/humanitarian associations. Subsidies: Allocations of support for public companies for the production of electric power companies and the agricultural sector, and the rest of public sector companies. Interest: Interest on public debt, remittances, bonds, and external debt. Other expenses: Emergency reserves, Kuwait war compensation, various debt settlements, and compensation.

percent (excluding pension), whereas the average for the comparator countries during this same period was between 5 and 15 percent (figure 2.6). By comparison, Turkey averaged around 6 percent, while the Arab Republic of Egypt averaged 7 percent. Jordan's six-year average was higher at 13 percent.

The adoption of the pay scale in 2004 raised the salaries of government employees by ID 1,065 million annually. This resulted in public sector wages becoming four to five times higher than private sector wages.[5] Also, increasing public sector employment as a result of indiscriminate hiring, starting from early-2000s, has expanded the wage bill.

According to the 2007 World Bank policy note, staffing of the public sector increased from 1.2 million in 2003 to approximately 2.8 million in 2007, with just over 2 million employed as civilians (including some 623,000 teachers), approximately 263,000 in the armed forces, and at least 500,000 working in state-owned enterprises. The exact number of public sector employees needs to be further detailed according to establishment, pay and grading, age structure, and

Figure 2.5 High Oil Prices/Revenues Translate into High Wage Bill, 2005–10

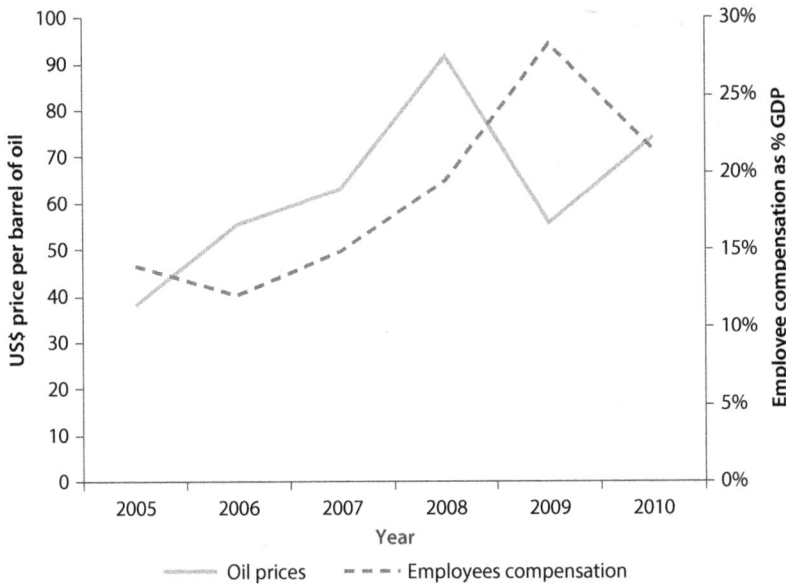

Source: World Bank, World Development Indicators, 2013.

Figure 2.6 Compensation of Employees, 2005–10

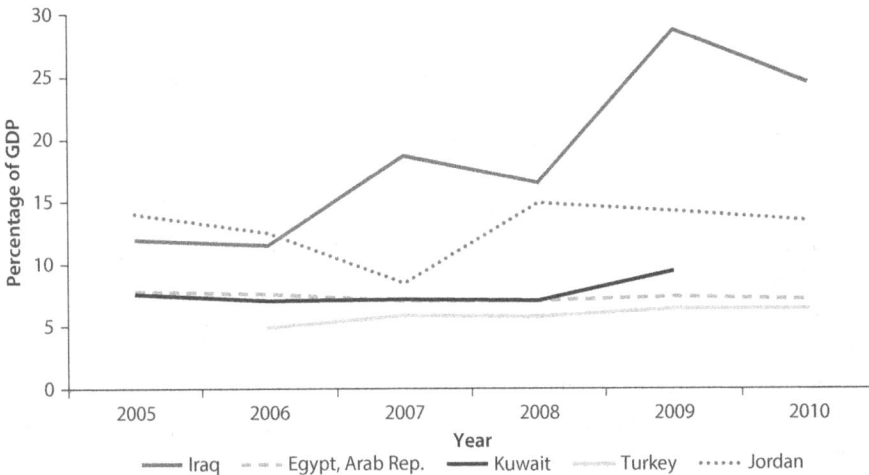

Source: World Bank, World Development Indicators, 2013.

geographical location at the central, regional, governorate, and district levels, (including the SOE level) in order for the government to plan for a much-needed functional restructuring. The 2012 budget presented the employment numbers by grades for ministries and centrally funded departments (appendix D).

There is evidence of considerable loss and waste through payroll and HR practices. Audit reports indicate that significant resources are being wasted through the payroll by a variety of inappropriate practices, including "ghost workers" and "double dippers." A World Bank policy note estimated the potential cost to the government to be as much as US$260 million a year.[6] The fragmented anecdotal evidence indicates that the problem could be much greater than what is presented here. For example, one of the audit results showed that 8,206 guards were listed on a payroll, but only 603 people were doing work that could be identified and counted. The 2011 Board of Supreme Audit (BSA) review found that the employees at the Council of Representatives, who reached the mandatory retirement age (63 years), had not been retired, in violation of paragraph four of the Ministry of Finance Publication No. 8373 on February 19, 2009.

Similarly, in the KRG, the public sector is too large and costly. The civil service in the KRG was composed of 586,502 employees in 2007, divided into 40 ministries, and a number of independent agencies.[7] Total public sector employment in KRG accounts for about 14.3 percent of the population and 24 percent of the total labor force. This ranks well above the regional average. Employee compensation increased from ID1.5 trillion in 2006 to ID2.4 trillion in 2010. The administration is characterized by opaque employment practices. There is no clear process for hiring, evaluation, and promotion. The 2008 Ernst & Young report suggested that KRG payroll and HR practices lead to significant waste of public resources.

Several international organizations have undertaken investigative work on payroll reform in Iraq, including the World Bank, IMF, International Advisory and Monitoring Board (IAMB), and others. The following specific problems in payroll management have been identified: (i) there are no common payroll applications or data formats between ministries; (ii) audit functions generally check month-on-month variances, rather than random or compliance checks; (iii) disbursement processes are weak; (iv) there are instances of managers collecting salaries on behalf of employees; (v) post-payroll accounting is uniformly weak; and (vi) validation of payments exhibits signs of structural weaknesses.

It is vitally important for the Iraqi government's long-term fiscal position that the wage bill growth is contained. Handled properly, an effective and well-functioning payroll system will lay the groundwork for Iraq's broader effort, protected in Article 105 in the Constitution, to establish an independent meritocratic civil service. Progress in wage containment and payroll reform will be linked to the government's ability to advance on broader issues such as implementing robust budget ceilings, reducing patronage and enhancing meritocracy in recruitment or promotion, strengthening internal audit capacity, or drafting new civil service legislation.

In laying out the Iraqi government's program for 2011–14, the prime minister has identified civil service reform as one of the key areas. In a message sent to Parliament in August 2011, the prime minister presented the vision to reform the public administration system and to reach good governance through the following actions: (i) reform of the civil service system, adoption of the Civil Service Law, and the establishment of the Federal Civil Service Council; (ii) review of legislation and regulations; (iii) institutional reform and review of organizational structures, internal regulations, job descriptions, and staffing requirements; (iv) reform of the practices of public financial management; (v) improvement of communication between government institutions, and between the federal government and local government institutions; and (vi) strengthening of anticorruption measures and continued cooperation with international organizations combating corruption and bilaterals. It is now time to move to implementation.

Operation and Maintenance

Reflecting pervasive inefficiencies and waste, purchase of other goods and services, the second largest recurrent expenditure, are also unusually high. They accounted for on average 14 percent of total expenditure (or 9 percent of GDP) between 2005 and 2010 (MTFF 2013–15). Key spending items included imports of drugs; imports of electricity, kerosene (for KRG), and fuel for power generation; costs associated with exports of crude oil; and purchase of other goods and services (that is, for Ministries of Interior and Defense). Although it constitutes a significant share, spending on goods and services has remained almost flat over the period. Utility and services charges to consumers are well below the cost of delivery.

Social Transfers and Consumer Subsidies

Social benefits, pensions, and subsidies together accounted for slightly over 20 percent of total expenditure (or 13 percent of GDP) between 2005 and 2010. According to the 2013–15 MTFF data, social benefits to households, delivered in the form of ration card (Public Distribution System) accounted for 11.2 percent of total public expenditure (or 6.1 percent of GDP); pensions for 6.8 percent of total expenditure; and subsidies for another 3.7 percent of total expenditure. Iraq's social protection system goes beyond the "ration card," and includes displaced relief and aid, social protection networks, and subsidies (agriculture, electricity, industry, and minerals subsidies), including KRG. Reforming the social benefits, pensions, and subsidies offers another potential opportunity in terms of Iraq's ability to reorient greater spending toward capital investment and social sector services (such as health and education). The Iraqi government needs to implement a well-designed social protection program that can limit social and political impacts of removing subsidies.

   High transfers and subsidies run the risks of turning the country into a rentier economy. The PDS continues to act as a cushion that provides a large transfer to poor households, keeping them out of deep poverty, but it is very costly and inefficient, as food rations are provided to wealthy as well as poor households.[8] Food subsidies maintain a vital safety net for all of the population, but undermine agriculture and distort domestic food markets. The PDS management is rudimentary, making it vulnerable to waste, theft, and corruption. Calculations suggest that it costs more than US$6 to transfer US$1 worth of food to a poor beneficiary (World Bank 2005).

   The Public Distribution System represents an unsustainable cost to the Government of Iraq. The PDS budget allocation was reduced from US$6.9 billion

Table 2.2 Budget: Subsidies, Social Benefits, and Pensions, 2005–12

ID billions, unless otherwise indicated

	2005 Estimated Actuals	2006 Estimated Actuals	2007 Estimated Actuals (BSA)	2008 Estimated Actuals (BSA)	2009 Estimated Actuals (MOF)	2010 Estimated Actuals (MOF)	2011 Forecast Actuals	2012 Original Budget
TOTAL EXPENDITURES	26,610	31,625	31,701	56,032	54,661	53,905	62,589	69,171
of which:								
Subsidies	268	677	1,514	3,623	1,572	2,557	3,319	1,148
Subsidies (as a share of total budget)	1.0	2.1	4.8	6.5	2.9	4.7	5.3	1.7
Subsidies (in percent of GDP)	0.6	0.9	2.1	3.5	2.1	2.7	2.6	0.8
Social Benefits	5,304	4,529	5,755	9,257	5,660	5,144	5,156	5,629
of which: Public Distribution System	5,299	4,519	2,039	6,986	4,200	3,500	3,577	4,088
PDS (as a share of total budget)	19.9	14.3	6.4	12.5	7.7	6.5	5.7	5.9
PDS (in percent of GDP)	11.5	6.2	2.9	6.8	5.6	3.7	2.8	2.9
Pensions and Other Retirement Benefits	2,765	2,608	2,299	2,854	3,293	6,252	6,382	7,339
Pensions (as a share of total budget)	9.0	7.0	5.8	4.2	6.0	8.9	7.2	7.3
Pensions (in percent of GDP)	6.0	3.6	3.2	2.8	4.4	6.6	4.9	5.3

Source: MTFF, 2013–15.

Note: BSA = Board of Supreme Audit; GDP = gross domestic product; MOF = Ministry of Finance.

in 2008 to US$4.1 billion in 2012; however, it is still high. Its high cost in budget might have led to some crowding out of other social spending.[9]

The PDS has suffered challenges regarding the quality and quantity of items, inefficiencies in the distribution system, and sometimes limited access to the population due to the lack of security. The main aspects of inefficiencies include: (i) weaknesses in procurement and financial management, which leave the system vulnerable to waste, theft, and corruption; (ii) lack of targeting of the food rations to the poorest segments of Iraq's population; (iii) the high dependence on the PDS as a major source of food is inherently a source of vulnerability, as disruptions in food distribution often lead to acute food insecurity; and (iv) the food items in the basket are mostly imported; and the food baskets have been heavily subsidized—they are virtually free.[10]

The Government of Iraq has already taken important steps toward reforming subsidies and safety nets. Direct budgetary fuel subsidies were eliminated in 2008, except for a small subsidy on kerosene. A targeted cash-based safety net has been expanded. The PDS reform is under implementation.

As a next step, the Government of Iraq, with the National Development Plan (NDP), has committed to substantially reforming, and eventual monetizing, of the PDS. The Council of Ministers (CoM) following the recommendations of the poverty reduction strategy (PRS) 2010–14, has approved a plan presented by the government's High Committee for PDS Reform that contains the detailed actions to be taken to implement the PRS.[11] This includes a phased five-year plan to reduce the number of PDS beneficiaries to cover only the poor population by 2015 and, in parallel, an expansion and improvement in the services provided through social safety nets (SSNs) (figure 2.7). The government's 2010 Budget Law has requested the Ministry of Trade (MoT) to develop a detailed plan to reform the PDS. MoT signed a Memorandum of Understanding with the World Food Program in November 2009 for a two-year (2010–12) project titled

Figure 2.7 Plan for Phasing Out of Public Distribution System and Phasing in of Social Safety Net System, 2010–14

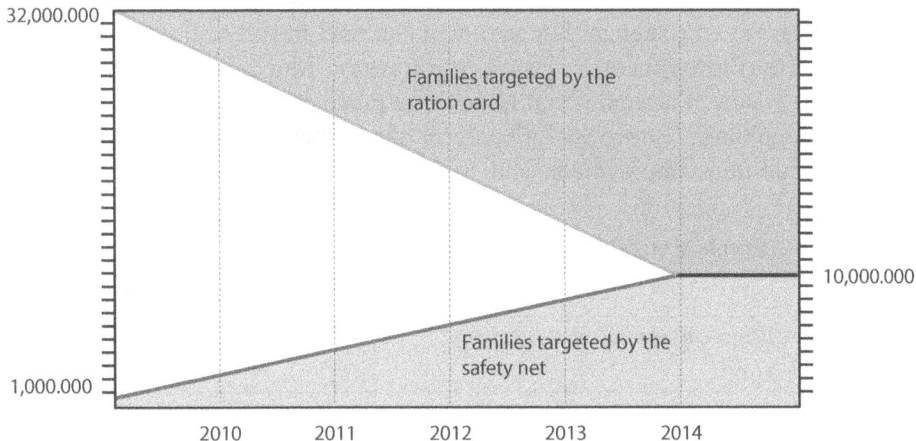

Source: Iraq Ministry of Planning.

"Capacity Development for Reforming the PDS and Strengthening Social Safety Nets for Vulnerable Groups" to support the reform of the PDS and improve efficiency in managing the supply chain (FAO 2011).

The World Bank is supporting a four-part program in reforming the PDS: (i) gradually introducing targeting; (ii) reducing the number of products in the ration basket; (iii) increasing the role and capacity of the private sector in the PDS, and in food markets in general; and (iv) improving procurement and financial management. The World Bank is helping the government with the PDS targeting methodology, rollout of the PDS targeting exercise and communication strategy.[12]

Transfer to Enterprises and Producer Subsidies

Transfers to SOEs have been high. The Federal Budget continues to allocate significant amounts over the last years for SOEs (table 2.3). These funds have been mainly used for covering SOE salaries and other employment benefits. Essential service-delivering sectors such as health, education, water, and sanitation have been allocated annual funds that were less than the amounts transferred for nonperforming SOEs.[13] In addition, there are other hidden and off-budget forms of SOE finances. For example, in 2006 and 2007, it is believed that a part of the "Advances Account" which reached ID 12 trillion was used to pay for SOE wages. In 2008 and 2009, SOE wages were paid through loans exceeding ID 2 trillion. The 2010 Budget includes loan guarantees, with the Ministry of Finance (MoF) instructing state-owned banks to lend to SOEs against "viable business plans and feasibility studies." Furthermore, SOEs are maintaining large balances at state-owned banks, which are beyond the scrutiny and control of the Ministry of Finance.

SOEs in Iraq include a large variety of public entities, including ministries, directorates/departments, and bodies. SOEs are structured in various holdings, regional branches, and factories. There are 177 SOEs, distributed among ministries, with the Ministry of Industry & Minerals holding the largest share (67), followed by Oil (16), Finance (13), and Construction and Housing (11).

While many SOEs have restarted operations after years of damage and looting, a significant number remain inoperable. However, many continue to keep workers on the payroll even though they are not operational and are not producing goods or services. Employment by SOEs, according to MoF's Federal Budget Law FY2010, stands at around 633,000, twice as much as that recorded in 2005. In Iraq, the public sector provides 43 percent of total jobs and almost 60 percent of overall full-time employment, and the employees in state-owned companies

Table 2.3 Transfers to State-Owned Enterprises

	2007	*2008*	*2009*	*2010*
Transfers to state-owned enterprises (US$ million)	905	2,560	2,906	2,564
Percentage of GDP	1.6	2.7	4.4	3.2

Source: Ministry of Finance, Budget Execution Reports.

make up about 20 percent of total public employment. In the Ministry of Industry and Minerals, about 37 percent of the employees are considered to be above ideal staffing levels.[14] The private sector accounts for 25 percent of part-time employment with wages being lower than in public sector jobs. The dominant public sector in Iraq is hindering the development of market mechanisms and fair competition rules by way of large-scale interventions. Little progress has been made in implementing a civil service reform.

Producer subsidies have taken a substantial share from the budget between 2007 and 2011. For fuels, official prices at the pump are below operating costs. This encourages smuggling, black market dealings and corruption, and reduces the ability to self-finance refineries' rehabilitations. In the electricity sector, fuel for generators is below opportunity cost[15] and charges to consumers are below the cost of delivery. In the agriculture sector, seeds, fertilizers, fuel power, and equipment are at very low official prices. Agricultural subsidies in Iraq consist of (i) inputs and equipment at subsidized prices; (ii) crops brought at government-set prices; and (iii) storage, marketing, and processing arrangements.

As a positive development, the "Iraq Task Force for Economic Reforms" prepared a "Roadmap for Restructuring State-Owned Enterprises in Iraq" with the assistance of the United Nations and the World Bank. The mandate is to formulate a national SOE Restructuring Roadmap, along with a feasible phased action plan, which will be integrated into the governmental agenda for economic diversification and inclusive growth. The reform of SOEs aims at having government subsidies and financing over the public budget, whether federal or local, terminated in the course of restructuring, while the costs of all operations will be covered through enterprise revenues based on sound commercial principles.

As of 2010, the policy of the Ministry of Finance regarding the budget support for SOEs has changed, with SOEs being encouraged to apply for loans from state banks, conditional upon the submission of "viable business plans and feasibility studies" as stipulated in the Federal Budget Law for FY2010.

Grants and Other Expenditure
Grants and other expenditure together accounted for 15 percent of total expenditure (or 9 percent of GDP). "Other expenditure" is predominantly made up of the Kuwait war compensations, although this category also includes debts settlements abroad and other small expenditures. Grants constituted 5 percent of total expenditure (or 3 percent of GDP) and included contributions to regional and international institutions, foundation grants, grants to Baghdad and other municipalities, and grants to companies and public agencies. Interest payments and net acquisition of financial assets each accounted for about one percent of total expenditure.

Capital Expenditure
Following the international embargo and war, Iraq has rightfully prioritized the reconstruction of its infrastructure and the development of its resource potential. Public investment in Iraq has averaged 17 percent of total expenditure, or about

Table 2.4 Economic Composition of Government Expenditure, 2005–11

ID billion, unless otherwise indicated

	2005		2006		2007		2008		2009		2010		2011
	Original Budget	Estimated Actuals	Original Budget	Estimated Actuals	Original Budget	Estimated Actuals (BSA)	Original Budget	Estimated Actuals (BSA)	Original Budget	Estimated Actuals (MOF)	Original Budget	Estimated Actuals (MOF)	Original Budget
Compensation for Employees	**5,538**	**6,421**	**8,365**	**8,739**	**10,296**	**13,369**	**12,695**	**20,081**	**21,280**	**21,643**	**23,264**	**20,633**	**28,032**
of which:													
Defense	839	—	1,371	—	1,819	1,606	2,009	2,194	2,364	2,284	2,720	2,607	4,070
Public Order and Safety	1,125	—	2,355	—	2,807	3,297	4,068	4,396	5,835	5,301	6,363	5,256	6,969
Education	1,582	—	1,953	—	2,488	—	2,869	4,592	6,337	6,910	6,334	6,026	8,427
KRG	1,049	—	1,509	—	1,500	—	1,500	2,789	2,701	3,406	3,211	2,382	3,870
Pensions and Other Retirement Benefits	**2,552**	**2,765**	**3,976**	**2,608**	**3,924**	**2,299**	**4,357**	**2,854**	**4,598**	**3,293**	**5,644**	**6,252**	**6,382**
of which:													
KRG	331	—	348	—	300	—	300	—	690	—	727	1,668	953
Use of Goods and Services	**7,129**	**6,935**	**11,033**	**7,698**	**8,012**	**4,913**	**7,874**	**8,091**	**9,167**	**4,955**	**11,818**	**10,260**	**12,226**
of which:													
KRG	433	—	371	—	275	—	200	—	1,174	1,149	1,525	2,220	815
Interest	**150**	**86**	**486**	**438**	**551**	**620**	**760**	**670**	**689**	**385**	**1,072**	**917**	**1,416**
Subsidies	**499**	**268**	**1,634**	**677**	**1,726**	**1,514**	**2,326**	**3,623**	**3,432**	**1,572**	**2,904**	**2,557**	**1,093**
of which:													
Agriculture Subsidies	300	241	—	176	—	307	633	—	334	34	390	269	642
Electricity Subsidies	—	—	—	—	—	500	463	299	1,348	1,109	1,600	1,666	—
Industry and Minerals Subsidies	—	—	—	—	—	—	—	—	853	—	77	13	—
KRG Subsidies	—	—	197	—	200	—	235	190	286	286	300	300	293
Other Subsidies (General Public Services)	—	—	1,437	502	1,526	608	933	3,623	184	15	219	38	159

table continues next page

Table 2.4 Economic Composition of Government Expenditure, 2005–11 (continued)

ID billion, unless otherwise indicated

	2005		2006		2007		2008		2009		2010		2011
	Original Budget	Estimated Actuals	Original Budget	Estimated Actuals	Original Budget	Estimated Actuals (BSA)	Original Budget	Estimated Actuals (BSA)	Original Budget	Estimated Actuals (MOF)	Original Budget	Estimated Actuals (MOF)	Original Budget
Grants	1,877	1,262	4,690	1,673	2,184	1,585	2,020	6,432	2,234	1,739	2,434	3,046	4,790
of which:													
KRG	—	—	704	—	350	—	200	317	266	303	233	357	166
Social Benefits	6,000	5,304	5,705	4,529	5,576	5,755	5,572	9,257	5,603	5,660	5,135	5,144	5,508
of which:													
Public Distribution System	6,000	5,299	5,280	4,519	4,106	2,039	3,928	6,986	4,200	4,200	3,500	3,500	4,000
Displaced Relief and Aid	—	—	63	—	70	—	81	279	90	96	200	198	201
KRG Social Protection Network	—	—	105	—	429	—	429	230	196	195	250	242	323
Other Social Benefits[a]	—	—	160	—	68	1,040	870	853	193	182	8	1,112	892
Other Expenditure	3,516	3,570	4,220	5,263	5,733	3,944	5,442	7,875	5,744	3,423	6,156	5,098	7,507
of which:													
Kuwait War Compensations	1,285	1,730	2,127	2,235	—	2,380	3,645	—	2,154	—	2,803	—	3,587
Payment of Oil Treasury Money Orders	273	—	—	—	—	—	—	—	1,438	—	—	—	—
Debts Settlement Abroad	27	189	27	550	—	—	480	—	834	—	314	—	—
Emergency Reserve with KRG	—	—	—	—	484	484	700	—	489	—	585	—	—
Net Acquisiton of Non-Financial Assets	1,162	457	1,582	592	2,284	1,018	3,129	1,867	1,382	636	2,458	708	1,537
Total Recurrent Budget	28,423	27,066	41,691	32,217	40,286	32,720	44,174	56,032	54,129	43,306	60,886	54,613	68,491
Investment Expenditures	7,559	3,765	9,272	5,277	12,665	6,589	18,436	11,244	15,047	9,261	24,944	15,602	30,066
Grand Total	35,981	30,831	50,963	37,494	52,952	39,308	62,610	67,276	69,176	54,661	85,831	70,216	98,557

Source: MTFF, 2013–15.

a. Other social benefits classified administratively under Human Rights, Local Councils in the Provinces, Labor and Social Affairs, Secretariat to the Council of Ministers, and Council of Ministers Presidency.

Table 2.5 Public Investment Budget, 2005–10

ID billion

	2005	2006	2007	2008	2009	2010
Oil	4,500	5,300	3,000	3,543	2,604	3,104
Electricity	440	1,150	1,745	1,990	1,278	4,194
Water resources	276	300	330	450	680	1,153
Municipalities and public work	252	356	425	500	566	1,547
Health	60	50	431	200	482	1,140
Education	100	22	366	481	213	504
Higher education	50	60	259	255	213	412
Transportation	145	155	123	300	383	450
Housing and reconstruction	365	470	422	420	542	771
Industry and minerals	7	14	42	430	595	921
Communications	200	248	193	300	255	393
Kurdish Regional Government	750	750	1,966	3,047	2,303	3,438
Total	7,559	9,272	12,665	18,436	15,047	24,944

Source: Iraq Ministry of Planning.
Note: Transfers for provinces are included in the grand total but are not presented in the table.

10 percent of GDP, between 2005 and 2010. Although rising, Iraq's public investment is suffering from inefficiency and lack of effectiveness. General public services and economic affairs together accounted for well over three-quarters of total capital expenditure over 2005–10. A further unbundling of the general public services shows that nearly 40 percent went to "transfers between different levels of government" for payments to KRG and provincial and local governments. This category is still hard to pin down in terms of what the investment actually financed. Public investment in fuel and energy, and housing and community development, together accounted for nearly 40 percent of the total capital expenditure over 2005–10. On the other hand, capital investment in agriculture, mining, manufacturing and construction, and transport and communication together accounted for a relatively small share of less than three percent in total expenditure (or 0.3 percent of GDP). Capital expenditure saw a rise as a share of total expenditure during the period, and in terms of growth, most of the increases went to general public services (transfers between governments), fuel and energy, and housing and community development.

Fuel and energy sectors have received the highest allocations. Between 2005 and 2010, the highest share of the capital budget was spent on transfers between different levels of government (38 percent) followed by fuel and energy (24 percent), housing and community development (14 percent), and general public services (10 percent).

In the 2011 Investment Budget, road network activity represented 24.3 percent of the year's entire amended allocation to the transport and communications sector, **an increase of 38.4 percent over the proposed allocation.** This increase includes

Table 2.6 Sector Allocations, by Activity in the 2011 Budget: Transport and Communications Sector
ID million

Activity	Total cost	Proposed allocation	Amended allocation	Relative weight (%)
Road network	2,847,035.950	308,000.000	426,391.950	24.3
Traffic management	866,650.000	133,150.000	165,220.650	9.4
Road transport	131,600.000	31,850.000	37,729.007	2.2
Railway lines	5,541,000.000	155,850.000	234,393.819	13.4
Water transport	634,943.611	106,850.000	228,949.613	13.1
Air transport	190,427.000	29,200.000	62,191.410	3.6
Communications	1,898,130.000	249,500.000	469,590.000	26.8
Storage	116,955.000	10,000.000	34,627.857	2.0
Reconstruction	316,900.000	39,650.000	86,897.886	5.0
Media	15,010.000	2,500.000	8,304.000	0.5
Total	12,558,651.600	1,066,550.000	1,754,296.190	100.0

Source: Ministry of Planning, Department of Government Investment Programs, Investment Budget Section.

projects for highways and arterial roads linking governorate centers with borders, secondary roads, and rural roads. Railway activity represents 13.4 percent of the year's entire amended allocation for this sector, an increase of 50.4 percent over the proposed allocation. Water transport activity represents 13.1 percent of the year's entire amended allocation, with projects focusing on the upgrade of ports and quays and the purchase of steamboats. The overall transport and communications sector allocations amounted to ID 1,754.3 billion, which represents 5 percent of total investment projects, with an increase of 64.5 percent over the proposed allocations. This is due to the reallocation of funds remaining from 2010 and the transfer of ID 24.2 billion from the Ministry of Oil allocation to the oil ports support project being implemented by the Ministry of Transport.

The government is encouraging international companies to invest in the infrastructure sector. In February 2012, Iraq's Transport Minister appealed to international companies to help restore Iraq's infrastructure by rebuilding airports and constructing a European-style rail network. The government plans to renovate already-built airports and sea ports, as well as building new ones, and also plans to establish 2,000 kilometers of rail track. Iraq's 2012 budget allocates around US$1 billion for transport and communications. The cost and annual appropriations of ongoing transport projects are presented in appendix H.

Despite this clear emphasis, the country's infrastructure needs are still great. For example, to substantially increase production in the petroleum sector, significant investments will be required along the country's export routes, particularly in the Basra port area and along the northern pipeline between Kirkuk and Ceyhan. In the south, the needs are broad, including a new pipeline to connect exiting supplies to refineries, the construction of storage facilities, and port expansion. In the north, pipelines will require significant repair, and border stations will require new or renovated pumping and metering facilities. In the long-term, a more extensive gas infrastructure will be required in order for Iraq to tap into gas pipeline routes in Turkey that feed European markets. Also, Iraq is committed to making massive improvements in its refining capacity over the next decade. Currently, the country's refinery network is outdated and incapable of meeting growing domestic demand. In the electricity sector, the power grid has been severely damaged. Rising demand, in combination with shortage of supply, has left the grid in the state of near collapse. Power generation barely meets half of the demand, leading to frequent blackouts. Water supply is affected by power blackouts, which hinder pumping and water filtration.

This is in part because, beyond good intentions, Iraq has been characterized by a chronic underexecution of its capital budget. Although capital spending allocations have increased since 2005, Iraq's ability to follow through on its budgeted capital spending programs has been low (figure 2.8). While Iraq has consistently spent more than 80 percent of its originally planned recurrent budget, it has spent only 50 to 60 percent of its capital budget. Iraq needs to work harder to rebuild and expand its administrative capacity, including restoring information systems and strengthening project approval processes.

There also has been a lack of systematic prioritization in Iraq's capital budgeting decisions. It would be desirable to raise the efficiency of the investment effort in Iraq, both to increase the overall investment rate and to provide much needed infrastructure. However, recent experience in scaling up investment in middle-income countries suggests greater attention needs to be paid to the institutional framework that underpins the provision of investment.[16] Boosting growth will require not only scaling up public investment, but also ensuring that spending is highly efficient. The next chapter will discuss these issues in greater depth.

Figure 2.8 Recurrent and Capital Budgets: Original Allocations and Actual Spending, 2005–12

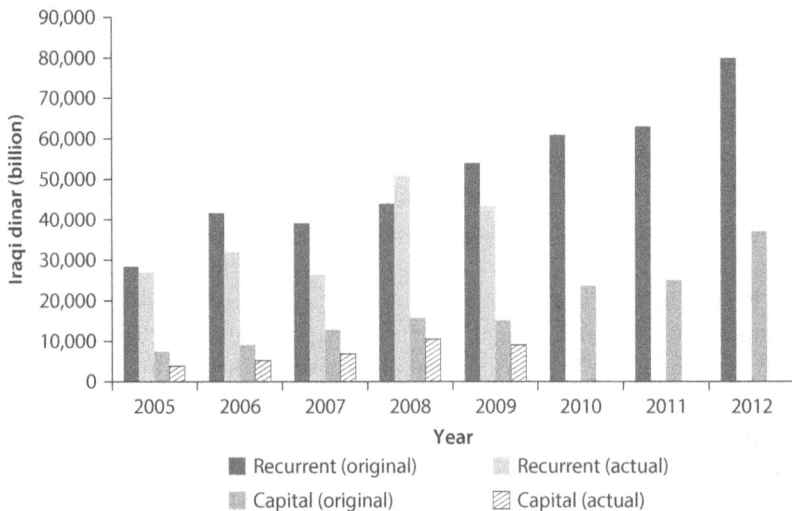

Source: MTFF, 2013–15.

Table 2.7 Functional Classification of Budget, by Recurrent and Capital Spending, 2005–11

as % of total

Iraq Budget: Total Expenditures by Functional Classification

(as % of total budget)

	2005 Original Budget	2005 Estimated Actuals (BSA)	2006 Original Budget	2006 Estimated Actuals (BSA)	2007 Original Budget	2007 Estimated Actuals (MOF)	2008 Original Budget	2008 Estimated Actuals (MOF)	2009 Original Budget	2009 Estimated Actuals (MOF)	2010 Original Budget	2011 Original Budget
General Public Services	18.9	26.8	41.7	31.4	31.4	21.1	30.1	27.7	28.0	27.6	29.6	30.1
Defense	5.6	—	10.1	1.7	10.1	12.9	10.7	7.0	7.2	6.9	6.9	6.9
Public Order and Safety	3.9	0.0	6.1	0.6	8.5	12.6	8.8	9.3	11.3	12.3	10.1	9.9
Economic Affairs	34.1	20.5	22.6	19.6	17.0	12.3	20.1	18.0	17.3	11.4	18.4	18.1
Environmental Protection	0.1	0.0	0.0	0.0	0.0	0.2	0.0	0.0	0.3	0.1	0.3	0.3
Housing and Community Development	3.0	1.2	2.7	1.0	2.8	0.3	2.6	3.5	3.4	3.5	4.9	4.9
Health	4.3	0.1	3.1	0.2	4.4	1.9	3.9	4.7	6.0	5.5	6.8	6.6
Recreation, Culture, Religion	0.9	0.3	0.4	0.2	0.6	0.9	1.0	1.1	1.7	1.2	2.2	2.2
Education	4.6	0.1	4.4	0.0	6.7	0.1	6.0	9.1	10.1	14.4	9.8	9.7
Social Protection	24.7	26.3	8.9	19.1	18.4	25.4	16.7	19.9	14.8	17.1	13.1	13.4
Total	100	100	100	100	100	100	100	100	100	100	100	100

table continues next page

Table 2.7 Functional Classification of Budget by Recurrent and Capital Spending, 2005–11 *(continued)*
as % of total

Iraq Budget: Recurrent Expenditures by Functional Classification
(as % of total budget)

	2005 Original Budget	2005 Estimated Actuals (BSA)	2006 Original Budget	2006 Estimated Actuals (BSA)	2007 Original Budget	2007 Estimated Actuals (MOF)	2008 Original Budget	2008 Estimated Actuals (MOF)	2009 Original Budget	2009 Estimated Actuals (MOF)	2010 Original Budget	2011 Original Budget
General Public Services	16.4	17.4	40.0	22.0	22.0	14.3	16.3	23.3	19.3	17.9	20.1	20.3
Defense	5.6	—	10.0	—	10.0	12.8	10.2	6.9	6.7	6.8	6.3	6.3
Public Order and Safety	3.6	—	5.9	—	8.3	12.6	8.5	9.2	10.9	12.0	9.7	9.5
Economic Affairs	19.2	19.1	9.0	18.5	6.8	9.2	11.6	9.8	9.5	8.3	8.1	7.6
Environmental Protection	0.0	—	0.0	—	0.0	0.2	0.0	0.0	0.3	0.0	0.2	0.2
Housing and Community Development	0.6	—	0.5	—	0.5	0.3	0.5	0.6	0.9	0.8	1.0	1.0
Health	4.1	—	3.0	—	3.6	1.9	3.8	4.6	5.3	5.0	5.5	5.2
Recreation, Culture, Religion	0.8	0.2	0.3	0.1	0.5	0.9	0.8	0.9	1.3	0.9	1.4	1.4
Education	4.2	—	4.2	—	5.4	0.1	5.4	8.1	9.5	13.7	8.8	8.6
Social Protection	24.6	26.3	8.9	19.1	18.4	25.4	16.6	19.9	14.8	17.1	13.1	13.4
Total	79.0	87.8	81.8	85.9	75.5	79.7	73.8	83.0	78.3	82.4	72.0	71.6

table continues next page

Table 2.7 Functional Classification of Budget by Recurrent and Capital Spending, 2005–11

as % of total

Iraq Budget: Capital Expenditures by Functional Classification

(as % of total budget)

	2005 Original Budget	2005 Estimated Actuals (BSA)	2006 Original Budget	2006 Estimated Actuals (BSA)	2007 Original Budget	2007 Estimated Actuals (MOF)	2008 Original Budget	2008 Estimated Actuals (MOF)	2009 Original Budget	2009 Estimated Actuals (MOF)	2010 Original Budget	2011 Original Budget
General Public Services	2.5	9.4	1.7	9.4	9.3	6.8	13.8	4.4	8.7	9.8	9.6	9.8
Defense	—	—	0.1	1.7	0.1	0.0	0.5	0.0	0.5	0.1	0.6	0.6
Public Order and Safety	0.3	0.0	0.2	0.6	0.2	0.0	0.3	0.1	0.4	0.3	0.4	0.4
Economic Affairs	14.9	1.4	13.6	1.1	10.3	3.1	8.5	8.2	7.8	3.0	10.3	10.5
Environmental Protection	0.0	0.0	0.0	0.0	0.0	—	0.0	0.0	0.0	0.0	0.0	0.0
Housing and Community Development	2.5	1.2	2.2	1.0	2.3	—	2.1	2.9	2.5	2.8	3.8	3.9
Health	0.2	0.1	0.1	0.2	0.8	—	0.2	0.1	0.7	0.5	1.3	1.4
Recreation, Culture, Religion	0.1	0.1	0.1	0.1	0.2	—	0.2	0.2	0.4	0.3	0.8	0.8
Education	0.5	0.1	0.2	0.0	1.3	—	0.6	1.0	0.7	0.7	1.0	1.1
Social Protection	0.0	—	0.0	—	0.0	—	0.0	0.0	0.0	0.0	0.0	0.0
Total	21.0	12.2	18.2	14.1	24.5	20.3	26.2	17.0	21.7	17.6	28.0	28.4

Source: MTFF, 2013–15.

Note: BSA = Board of Supreme Audit; MOF = Ministry of Finance; — = not available.

Functional Composition of Government Expenditure

Turning now to where Iraq spends its public monies, it appears that three items—general public services, social protection, and public order and safety—together account for well over 50 percent of Iraq's total public expenditure.

General Public Services

Reflecting how bloated the government is, the general public services budget item is by far the largest spending category, accounting for about a third of total public expenditure (or 17 percent of GDP) in Iraq. Included in this category are spending on the executive, legislative, and external affairs, public debt transactions, transfers of a general character between different levels of government, and other general services.

Defense and Security

Spending on defense and security is also disproportionately large. Defense and public order and safety (including police services, fire protection services, law courts, prisons, and other services) together accounted for 16 percent of total expenditure (or 9.2 percent of GDP). Given the current security situation, exceptional efforts may be needed. Still, even in such circumstances, policy makers should make sure that none of their resources go to waste. As Iraq gains stability and security over time, opportunities may exist for further budgetary savings over the medium- to long term, with this component providing fiscal room for further reorientation of spending toward capital investment or social services.

Economic Affairs

Economic affairs is another big spending item, accounting for 18 percent of total expenditure, the bulk of which constitutes spending on fuel and energy. Fuel and energy accounted for 11 percent of total expenditure (or 6.6 percent of GDP). Other key components of economic affairs—agriculture, mining, manufacturing and construction, and transport and communication—together accounted for a relatively small share of less than 2 percent of total expenditure.

Support for agriculture is a case in point. Iraq is heavily dependent on imported food to satisfy local demand. The country faces a number of challenges in the agriculture sector. Iraq's agriculture sector is under increasing pressure to feed its population, which is growing at an annual rate of more than 2.8 percent. The country will need much more than the current US$5 billion to import basic food to meet the annual shortages, for as long as required by domestic production, to achieve sustained growth.[17]

The sector's low productivity and growth rates are attributable to (i) past policies when the government maintained artificially low food prices through price and production controls and marketing restrictions, combined with (ii) years of insufficient maintenance and funding, which have degraded agricultural services and physical infrastructure, particularly the irrigation network. Government policies in the agricultural sector have been characterized by the state determination to control and subsidize farm inputs (fertilizers, seeds, insecticides, farm equipment, and machinery) and prices of strategic crops. Problems in irrigation are severe: they range from widespread deterioration of irrigation infrastructure to poor operation and maintenance of the systems, inefficient water use, soil salinity, weak institutional support, and the lack of a regulatory framework for efficient use and pricing of irrigation water. Access to credit is difficult outside of government ad hoc subsidized credit programs: private capital investment resources are lacking, as are credit initiatives available to farmers. The near absence of institutional credit has made the cost of capital prohibitive for agricultural producers and has discouraged private investment. The rehabilitation and development of the Iraqi agriculture sector is a medium-/long-term aim, which can only be achieved through a coherent, coordinated effort based on two main pillars: policy improvements and investment projects including inter alia, and rehabilitation of support services and capacity building.

The National Development Plan (2010–14) proposes to address some of these shortcomings as it aims to develop a stable, competitive, and sustainable agriculture sector to enhance food security and rural incomes, generate rural employment, diversify economic growth, and protect the natural environment. It emphasizes the development of social and economic infrastructure, research and genetic improvements of plants and livestock, and support to the private sector by developing adequate financial markets and credit policies. It draws attention to the problems of international water rights and water allocation between competing uses, to the integrated and efficient management of water resources, to the need for increasing agricultural productivity through the introduction of improved technologies and modern extension methods, to the need for considering a rural development approach to raise the economic and social level of the rural population, and to the need for legal reforms concerning land management and tenure.

Initial steps have been taken but much more remains to be done. In 2011, amended investment budget allocations to the agricultural sector amounted to ID 2,303.5 billion. Amended allocations for dams, reservoirs, and control facilities accounted for 14 percent of the allocation to this sector, for the purpose of upgrading dams and reservoirs to achieve the optimum utilization of water resources. Millennium Development Goals (MDG) monitoring shows that despite the investments in the past, the water sector is hardly able to expand its services to a larger proportion of the population. Allocations were made for the construction of new dams for the storage of water. Moreover, ID 693.8 billion was allocated in 2011 to support research, study, and survey activities. The funds have been distributed to the governorates in accordance with relative priority and the agricultural potential of each. Special funds have been set up to provide interest-free loans to peasants and farmers engaged in fruit and date farming, and for the development of animal resources.

Social Protection
In contrast to economic affairs, spending on social protection—which includes old-age support (pensions), support to family and children, and social exclusion-related support—comes closer to international patterns. It accounted for slightly over 20

percent of total expenditure (and about 12 percent of GDP). The mandatory pension system is composed of two separate funds: (i) the State Pension System (SPS), which covers civil servants,[18] and (ii) the Pensions & Social Security Department (SSD), which covers workers in the private sector. Together, the two schemes cover around 17 percent of the working-age population (or more than 3 million contributors, of which around 130,000 are in the private sector). Both systems suffer from weak administrative capacity. As discussed above, Iraq's Public Distribution System has been effective as a poverty reduction program but it has been costly and inefficient.

Pension payments represent one of the largest budget items of social protection spending in Iraq. In 2010, pension payments represented already more than 4 percent of GDP. This is among the highest levels of spending in the region. Emergency policies that were implemented after April 2003 replaced regular pensions with emergency "flat" payments paid directly from the Ministry of Finance budget, with very limited contributions from current workers or firms. Since 2006, however, regular earnings-related pensions have again been paid to those who have retired.

The Iraqi pension system, post April 2003, is exposed to two different types of problems: (i) those emerging as a result of the war and the implementation of a series of emergency policies; and (ii) those that are inherent structural problems. For both SPS and SSD, administrative capacity is weak, the operating environment is difficult, and there is a lack of coordination across other entities. Institutional capacity is in the process of being improved, forming and equipping the current staff to properly manage a new integrated social security and pension system that is still ill-prepared to design and implement necessary reforms. The systems are in the process of being integrated in only one national system, under the National Board of Pensions (NBP). Both schemes are designed as defined benefit arrangement, with essentially pay-as-you-go (PAYG) financing.

Besides the organizational challenges, the technical ones are also numerous. The current pension schemes face problems in terms of efficiency, equity, financial sustainability, and coverage. The mathematical relationships between accrual rates, retirement ages, and contribution rates are not respected. Implicit rates of the return on contributions are above sustainable levels and compromise the long-term viability of the system, even in the absence of an aging population; pensions are only indexed ad-hoc. Dual system increases administration costs, affects the mobility of the labor force, and distorts the labor market. Less than half of the labor force in Iraq is covered by a mandatory pension system.

Iraq is now in the process of reforming and integrating its pension systems, with support from the World Bank under the Pension Reform Implementation Support Technical Assistance (PRISTA) project. PRISTA responded to the GoI's request for assistance to support pension reforms in Iraq and the implementation of the Unified Pension Law. PRISTA aims to provide comprehensive support on development of the institutional system for the newly established State Pension Fund (SPF), build key organizational functions within the SPF, and support staff capacity building.

Iraq's pension law, introduced in December 2007, provides for a defined benefit system. The law established the State Pension Fund to collect contributions and pay pension benefits. The law also calls for the merger of the public and private pension scheme. The Unified Law entailed reforms that aimed to modernize the public pension scheme and improve financial sustainability. It aimed to do this by redesigning the financing scheme that was originally funded from general budget to become a defined benefit scheme with pay-as-you-go financing. While the new law presents a significant improvement of the pension system in Iraq, there are substantial challenges in terms of the GoI's capacity to implement the law, and to ensure a comprehensive, affordable, equitable, and sustainable old-age income protection mechanism in Iraq.[19] The mandatory pension system in Iraq will cover only roughly one-fourth of the labor force, which is low from a social protection point of view, and is 10 percentage points below the already low average coverage rate in the Middle East and North Africa region.

Social Services and Housing

Overall, spending on social services and housing is also broadly in line with international practices. Education, health, and housing—services that are deemed critical for expanding opportunities and reducing poverty according to Iraq's NDP and PRS—together accounted for about 15 percent of total expenditure (or 8 percent of GDP). Iraq spent, on average, about 4 percent of GDP on education between 2005 and 2010, of which about two-thirds went to pre-primary and primary education, and a third to secondary and tertiary education. This was slightly lower than the average for the Middle East and North Africa region countries (5.5 percent) and the upper middle-income countries. On the other hand, health spending, at around 2 percent of GDP, is very low, about 2–3 percentage points below the average of upper-middle-income countries and 5–7 percentage points below the average of most of the high-income Organization for Economic Cooperation and Development (OECD) countries. Government spending on housing and community development accounted for just under two percent of GDP, with about two-thirds of that investment being expenditure on housing and the remaining one-third being expenditure on water supply.

At around US$90 however, Iraq fares poorly with respect to per capita health expenditure. Iraq spent between US$40 and US$120 per capita on health from 2005 to 2009, whereas Saudi Arabia spent between US$800 and US$1,150 during the same period. The average for upper-middle-income countries ranged between US$600 and US$800 and the average for the Middle East and North Africa region countries ranged between US$300 and US$400. República Bolivariana de Venezuela spent between US$500 and US$700, while Azerbaijan spent between US$350 and US$550. Furthermore, Iraq's budget execution rates in the health sector have been low. Iraq's public health expenditure as a percent of total government expenditure was around 4 percent between 2005 and 2008, with a slight increase to 5.5 percent in 2009. The average for upper-middle-income countries and the Middle East and North Africa regional average was around 9 percent over the 2005 to 2009 period. Compared to other resource-rich countries, Iraq fares poorly. For example, República Bolivariana de Venezuela and Saudi Arabia spent around 9 percent of their budget on health expenditures. For a detailed analysis of the Iraqi health sector, see chapter 5.

Iraq's public spending levels in education fare considerably better in comparative terms. As a percent of GDP, Iraq spent between 4 and 6 percent between 2005 and 2008, which was roughly comparable to the average amount spent by upper-middle-income countries. Moreover, in 2009, Iraq spent close to 9 percent of its GDP on education, a figure which was higher than both the higher-income OECD countries, which averaged around 5.5 percent of GDP, and the average for the Middle East and North Africa region countries, which averaged around 5 percent of GDP. Regarding other resource-rich countries, Saudi Arabia averaged around 6 percent, República Bolivariana de Venezuela averaged around 3.7 percent, and Azerbaijan averaged between 2 and 3 percent (figure 2.9).

As a percent of the budget, Iraq's expenditure on education was somewhat lower than other countries in the past. However, in recent years it has surpassed both the high-income OECD countries and the upper-middle-income countries (figure 2.10). The percent of expenditure that Iraq dedicates to education spending has increased from 5.3 percent in 2006 to close to 15 percent in 2009. As a comparison, OECD countries spent on average about 12 percent of their budget on education between 2005 and 2008, and upper-middle-income countries spent around 14 percent. The average for Saudi Arabia and the Middle East and North Africa region is slightly higher, at 20 and 19 percent respectively. The percent of

Figure 2.9 Education Expenditure as a Percentage of GDP, 2005–09

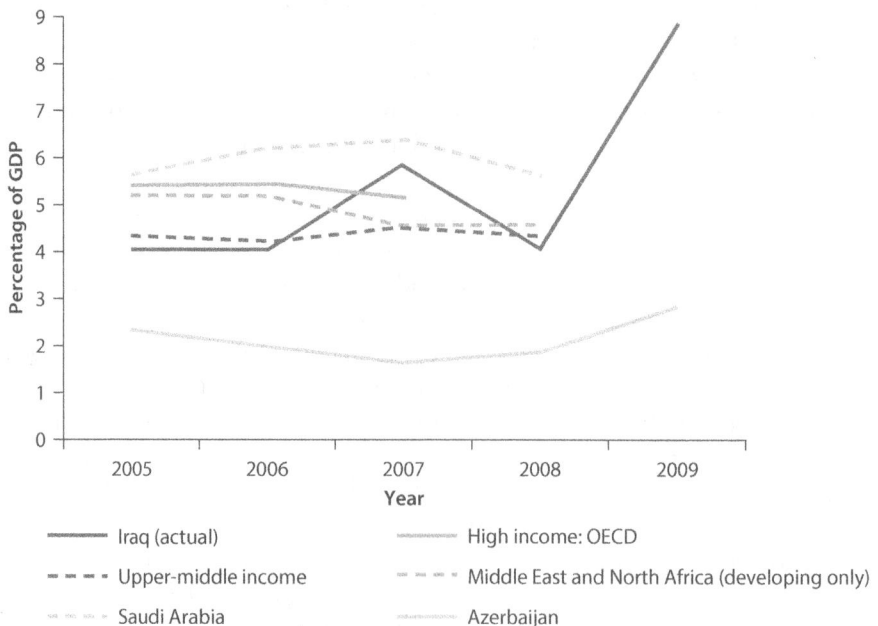

Source: World Bank, World Development Indicators, 2013.
Note: OECD = Organization for Economic Cooperation and Development.

Figure 2.10 Education Expenditure as a Share in Total Budget, 2005–09

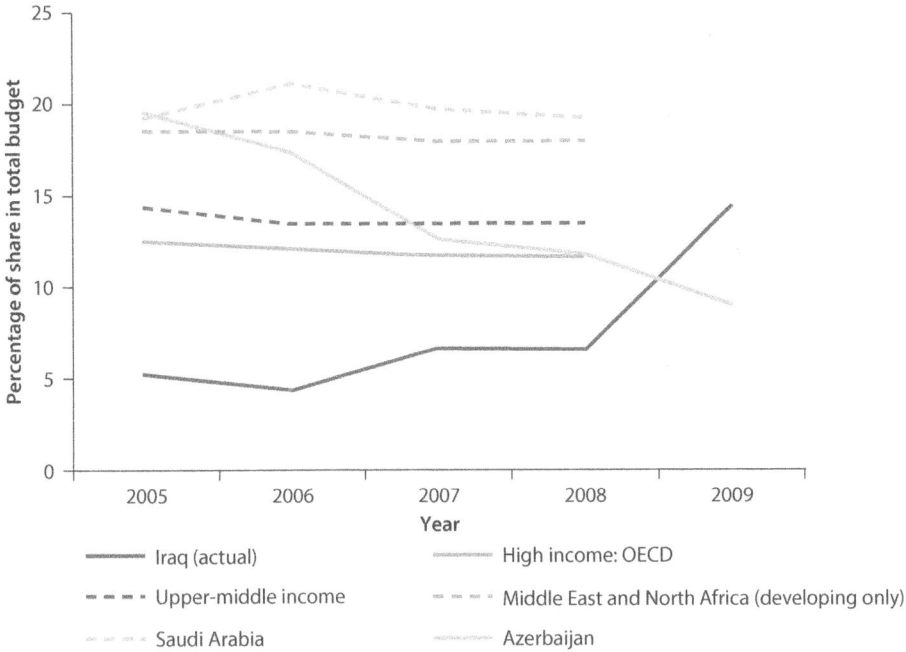

Source: World Bank, World Development Indicators, 2013.
Note: OECD = Organization for Economic Cooperation and Development.

Figure 2.11 Per Capita Education Expenditure, 2005–10

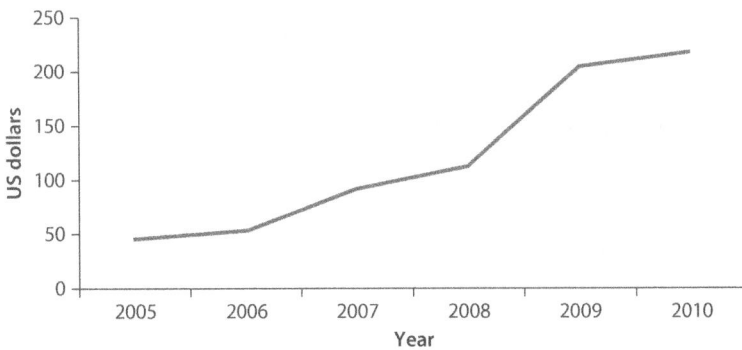

Sources: Iraqi Authorities; and World Bank World Development Indicators, 2013.

the budget that Azerbaijan dedicated to education has fallen from close to 20 percent in 2005 to around 9 percent in 2009.

Per capita education expenditure in Iraq has increased more than fourfold over the period, from less than US$50 per capita in 2005 to near US$220 per capita in 2010.

This is in part because, together with wages, education sector spending on teachers' salaries has been increasing. Trend analysis of the breakdown of education sector allocations and actual spending reveal that the major expenditure growth has been in resourcing for compensating public employees in the education sector (figure 2.12). Between 2007 and 2009, the cost of staffing salaries (and average cost of an education public servant) almost tripled, and is projected to increase further in the next two years. Staff remuneration constitutes the highest share in education spending, leaving little for quality-related inputs. Following the damage caused by years of neglect and conflict, many schools are in a state of disrepair, but considerable work is underway to construct and rehabilitate schools.

The growth in the cost of compensating education employees was driven by significant increases in numbers of public sector employees in the education sector

Figure 2.12 Education Sector Spending, 2005–14

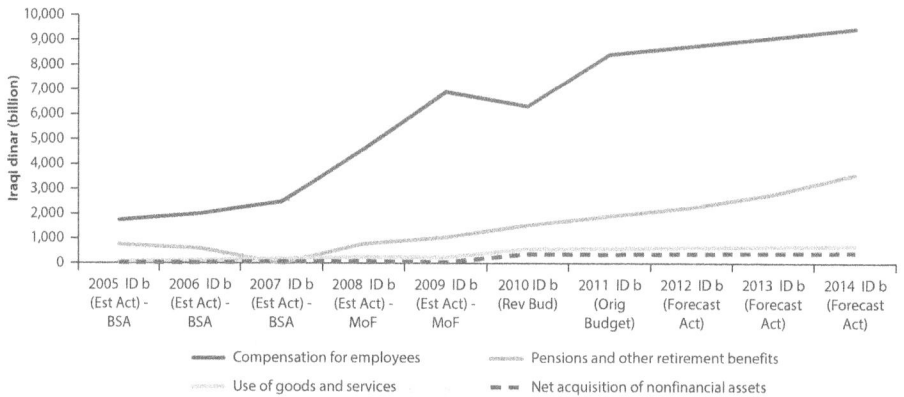

Source: MTFF, 2013–15.
Note: BSA = Board of Supreme Audit; MOF = Ministry of Finance.

Figure 2.13 Education Sector Staffing, 2005–11

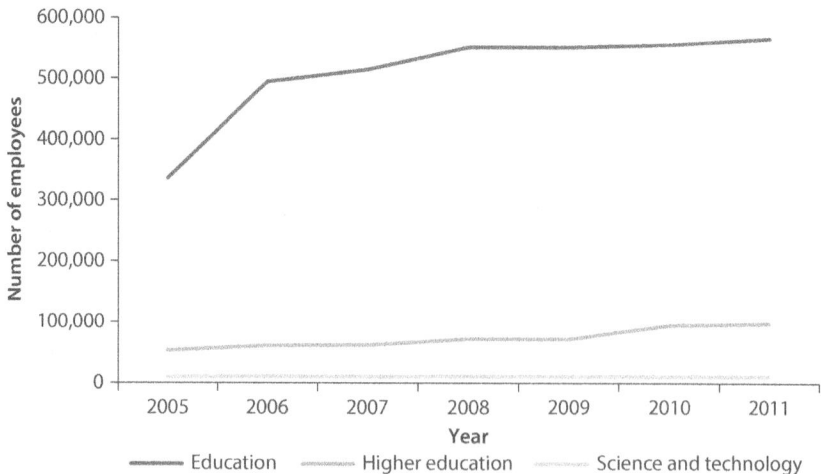

Source: Iraqi Authorities.

in 2006, and by salary increases through increment adjustments and rebasing. The Ministry of Education experienced a large increase in staffing numbers (64 percent) and the cost of compensating employees (156 percent) between 2005 and 2008. The cost of compensating employees almost doubled a year later.[20]

Table 2.8 reveals that the student to teacher ratio is approximately 20.[21] This indicates that the increase in staffing may have been based to some extent on growth in student numbers and target student-teacher ratios, though better pay for teachers appears to be the primary reason. The cost of compensating officials was due in part to reclassification policies related to job functions (that is, teachers being paid at a higher public service classification level and/or large rounds of

Figure 2.14 Ministry of Education Staffing Growth in Level 4 and Below, 2005–11

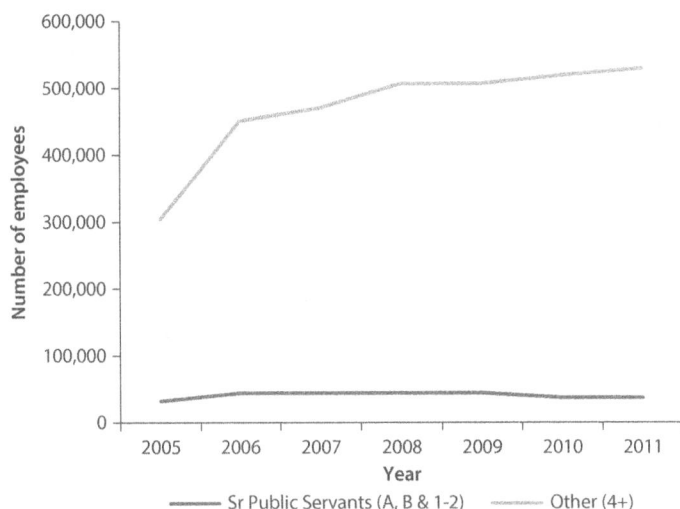

Source: Iraqi Authorities.

Table 2.8 Estimates of Students and Nontertiary Public Servants, 2005–11

	2005	2006 Est.	2007 Est.	2008 Est.	2009 Est.	2010 Est.	2011 Est.
Number of students (primary, secondary and tertiary)[a]	6,181,431	6,490,503	6,815,028	7,155,779	7,513,568	7,889,246	8,283,709
Primary education, pupils[a]	4,430,267	4,651,780	4,884,369	5,128,588	5,385,017	5,654,268	5,936,981
Secondary education, pupils	1,751,164	1,838,722	1,930,658	2,027,191	2,128,551	2,234,978	2,346,727
Tertiary	*n/a*	*n/a*	*n/a*	*n/a*	*n/a*	*n/a*	*n/a*
Cost per nontertiary student (US$)	201.27	199.28	199.13	219.40	198.75	173.00	252.73
Number of nontertiary public servants	336,592	494,594	514,644	551,089	*551,089*	556,164	566,164
Student/nontertiary public servant ratio	18	13	13	13	14	14	15

Source: Iraqi Authorities; WDI 2012; Global Development Finance (GDF) 2012; and author estimates.
a. Private-public splits not available at time of writing.

promotions). This, and other increases to pay scales, primarily account for the increase in the average cost of an education employee from around US$2,141 to US$9,071.

Overall, there are adequate numbers of teaching staff, but with shortages in some areas (both geographically and by subject). However, there is a lack of adequate planning for teacher supply and coordination between the Ministry of Education and Ministry of Higher Education and Scientific Research (MOHESR). The 2011 BSA report found that no education supervisors and specialists affiliated with the General Directorate of Education of Baghdad/First Rasafa had visited the schools during the school year 2008/09, and the oversight division at the General Education Directorate of the Governorate of Salah El Din has a severe shortage of supervisors.[22]

In 2011, the Iraqi government drafted the first education strategy in Iraq. The draft strategy includes all levels of education and all regions in Iraq. The strategy coincides with the MDGs and to date has been discussed with some stakeholders. Work is now under way on the implementation plans for the strategy. Basic statistical data are collected but there are some issues with the quality and reliability. Data reporting is uneven across ministries, and is challenging in general. The draft strategy envisages plans to increase funding for education. However, there is little emphasis on ensuring expenditures are equitably distributed across rural/urban areas and regions, on ensuring that social equity is taken into account, or on moving from item-based to program-based schemes. Furthermore, it is unclear whether the government will grant further authority to disburse funds at the school level.

Public Utilities

The water and sanitation sector is one of the examples of ineffective spending and inefficient service delivery. Despite recurrent and investment budget allocations to the Ministry of Water Resources (appendix B), because of the lack of an integrated budget, as well the as split in responsibilities between the Ministry of Municipalities and the Public Works and Municipality of Baghdad, the implementation of a coherent, least-cost allocation and investment strategy has been difficult.[23] This has resulted in a lack of attention to maintenance and operational efficiency. Salaries make up approximately 45 percent of the operational budget. Unless the poor collection rates and deteriorating collections are reversed, even large tariff increases will not compensate for lost revenue. The main causes of poor finances are insufficient tariffs, inadequate billing collections, and relatively high water loss. Tariff levels are very low and do not allow cost recovery to be achieved.

Access to services has been inadequate, particularly outside of Baghdad. There are no customer service units. Customers, particularly commercial ones, would be willing to pay for the service and increased costs if service delivery was improved. Eighty two percent of the population is served by sewerage or combined system and 70 percent are connected to the wastewater system. The water and sanitation sector needs to be customer oriented, and management efficiency needs to be improved in producing and delivering quality sector services.

Republic of Iraq Public Expenditure Review • http://dx.doi.org/10.1596/978-1-4648-0294-2

There is a need for a national policy for the water and sanitation sector in Iraq, which includes guidelines on how capital investments are to be managed and delivered, and how costs are to be recovered. Currently, the central government either directly or, through its departments in the governorates (except KRG), exercises its main functions, and structural units put into effect decisions with little management, power, or authority.[24] The strategy outlined in the Five-Year Strategic Development Plan for 2010–14 needs to be reviewed and assessed. The strategy proposed by the Ministry of Municipalities and Public Works (MMPW) only covers capital investment plans for 15 non-KRG governorates and the Municipality of Baghdad (MoB), and has them merely as a list of interventions. While the strategy describes the vision for the future, it does not set out how the vision is to be achieved. Moreover, the institutional framework of the water and sanitation sector in the MMPW and MoB is unclear, with overlapping functions, vague legal assignment of responsibilities, and inadequate control and enforcement mechanisms.

The case of the electricity sector is similar to that of water and sanitation. The electricity sector is covered in more detail in chapter 4.

Conclusions and Proposed Work

In summary, this chapter argues that allocative efficiency needs to improve significantly to reach fiscal discipline for effective service delivery. The following are four key recommendations:

• Manage oil revenues better. Create a sovereign "parking fund" and a fiscal stabilization fund to minimize the impact of oil revenue volatility on expenditure policy. Oil revenues could be housed under these funds until spending efficiency improves, but withdrawals would be guided by a medium term macro-fiscal policy framework, designed to provide support for a sustainable economic growth.
• Improve the strategic orientation and alignment of public expenditure by strengthening medium-term planning and fiscal framework. Link macro-fiscal policies to actual resource allocation decision making.
• Achieve greater fiscal consolidation and reorient a greater proportion of spending to capital investment, particularly through better control of the wage bill and reform of social benefits and subsidies.
• Increase the productivity and efficiency of present capital expenditure while creating more room for increased public investment.

The Bank can work with the government through the following proposed work to address the key issues:

Policy Note on Government Employment and Wage Bill. An analysis of the government employment and wage bill will be conducted to help identify possible payroll and civil service-related reforms. The overall wage bill will be analyzed and the structure of the wage bill across ministries and levels of the government will be presented. In addition, public sector employment will be reviewed to understand the sectoral pattern and composition of employment. To complement the efforts of the PER, under IFMIS component of the PFM project, the team could implement a "Payroll Control System" for an improved budget planning and effective budget execution controls over the wage bill.

This study will involve a mission to ascertain the structure of Iraq's payroll and employment structure, and the final policy note will provide policy recommendations to the Iraqi government on possible reform options.

A Policy Note on Fiscal Implications of Social Safety Nets. Another proposed output is a policy note on fiscal implications of Iraq's social safety net system. In particular, policy options could be discussed on how savings and fiscal reallocations would be coordinated from the planned phasing out of PDS and the phasing in of a cash-transfer-based SSN system.

Notes

1. Given Iraq's oil dependence and the volatility of oil revenues, macroeconomic variables expressed as a share of GDP need to be interpreted carefully. Because of the dominant role of the oil sector in Iraq's economy, nominal GDP is highly sensitive to changes in oil prices. Fluctuations in variables such as the public spending-to-GDP ratio to a large extent reflect changes in the denominator as opposed to changes in the numerator.

2. The DFI was introduced under UNSCR 1483/2003 as an account to deposit all Iraqi oil revenues and frozen assets. The MoF is in charge of managing the DFI account under Section V (*para.* 4.a) of the Financial Management Law.

3. The World Bank will soon complete a capacity development program with the Iraq BSA that aims to strengthen crucial audit practices.

4. Data refer to average share of actual budget as executed (reported by BSA for 2005–07 and by MoF for 2008–10).

5. Beschel Robert, Bill Monks, Mikhail Pryadilnikov, and Catherine Laurent (2007). Policy Note on "The Imperative of Wage Containment & Payroll Reform." World Bank, Washington, D.C.

6. Ibid.

7. Beschel Robert and David Biggs (August 2009). Policy Note on "Civil Service Reform in the KRG." World Bank, Washington, D.C.

8. The 2011 BSA audit found that as of May 2010, 4,939 government officials have been receiving subsidy from the safety net.

9. Concept note for a World Bank technical assistance on "Iraq: Rationalization of the Universal Public Distribution System," November 2010.

10. Iraq Agriculture Sector Note (2011). Paolo Luciani with contributions by Maurice Saade. Prepared under the Food and Agriculture Organization of the United Nations and the World Bank. FAO Investment Center.

11. The High Committee for PDS Reform has made some progress since 2010. The ration card is restricted to five items, namely flour, rice, vegetable oil, sugar, and baby milk. This commodity basket will be kept though 2012–14, and the quantity of allocations will be determined based on Iraq Household Socio-Economic Survey data and nutri-

tional requirements. On the other hand, the ration card has been discontinued for 350,000 households that has high income or are employed by the government.

12. World Bank Aide Memoire on Rationalization of the Public Distribution System Technical Assistance, June 2011.

13. Iraq Task Force for Economic Reforms (August 2010) with the assistance of the United Nations and the World Bank. Roadmap for Restructuring state-owned enterprises in Iraq. Baghdad, Iraq.

14. The Roadmap for Restructuring SOEs documented that 76 SOEs are under the authority of the Ministry of Industry and Minerals, consisting of 250 factories and over 200,000 employees, generating over 200 different products and services ranging from baby milk to cement to systems engineering.

15. World Bank (2006). Rebuilding Iraq: Economic Reform and Transition. Washington, D.C.

16. IMF, *Investing in Public Investment: An Index of Public Investment Efficiency*. Working Paper, December 2010.

17. Iraq Public Sector Modernization Program (2011). Key Findings and Recommendations: Education, Health, and Water & Sanitation, *Draft I-PSM Document*. UNDP, WHO, UNESCO, UNFPA, UNESCWA, UNICEF, UN HABITAT with the support of the European Union.

18. It also covers military and security personnel and employees in state-owned enterprises (SOEs).

19. Alkhoja Ghassan, and Zaina Dawani (December 2011). Pension Reform Implementation Support Technical Assistance (PRISTA): Institution Building in Iraq—The PRISTA Model. *MENA Knowledge and Learning Quick Note Series Number 50, World Bank.*

20. Staffing numbers for 2008 were not available at the time of writing; 2009 numbers were used as a preliminary estimate. Actual data for 2008 is likely to be lower.

21. Staffing splits between teachers, administrators, and ministry management was not available at time of writing.

22. The 2011 BSA report also found that some schools are unfit to be occupied. The Report pointed out that most of the buildings of the General Directorate of Education of Baghdad/First Rasafa need restoration, in addition to the fact that a number of vocational schools affiliated to the General Directorate for vocational education are unfit, and the number of schools is not commensurate with the number of students. The General Education Directorate of the governorate of Kerkuk still contains schools that are unfit to be occupied and in need of restoration, and some of them have not been operating since 1990.

23. Iraq Public Sector Modernization Program (2011). Key Findings and Recommendations: Education, Health, and Water & Sanitation, *Draft I-PSM Document*. UNDP, WHO, UNESCO, UNFPA, UNESCWA, UNICEF, UN HABITAT with the support of the European Union.

24. Ibid.

CHAPTER 3

From Strategy to Execution

Introduction

The previous chapter proposed an approach to make the best of the impending boom in oil revenues by shifting to a save and invest via curbing wages and subsidies and redirecting resources to public investment and basic services. The question is how to turn this aspiration into a reality on the ground, and make sure that the plans and strategies do not dissipate when the resource constraint is relaxed.

This has three dimensions:

(1) Connecting strategies to resource allocation
(2) Establishing sufficiently binding commitment devices to make sure that medium-term strategies "stick"
(3) Ensuring that resources saved for investment are indeed invested in valuable physical and financial assets and yield the hoped-for benefits for the population both in the short and in the long term.

Implementing these three dimensions will be critical for better service delivery to the Iraqi population. Currently, lack of fiscal discipline and weak links between strategies and budget execution bring challenges. Fiscal policy is not aligned with national priorities, and the goals identified in the National Development Plan (NDP) and poverty reduction strategy (PRS) are far from achieved. The government needs a mechanism to ensure that public expenditure can be realized as envisaged. At the same time, an effective public investment management framework is required in Iraq to strengthen the capacity for implementation of much needed infrastructure projects.

The chapter discusses these dimensions, and concludes with presenting the case for a comprehensive public investment management framework for Iraq, which will involve the Bank helping the government to undertake an institutional assessment of Iraq's public investment management system.

From Strategy to Resource Allocation

One of the challenges Iraq faces is the allocation of resources in accordance with strategic priorities. There has been no shortage of strategies in the past; however, linking a realistic set of strategies guided by a national vision to actual budget allocations has been weak. There has been some progress in addressing budget preparation and planning issues through the government's Public Financial Management Action Plan (PFMAP), and further work needs to be done to structure institutional arrangements for strategic allocation of resources and improve the quality of information needed to do this effectively.

This section reviews the links between the national strategies (National Development Plan and the poverty reduction strategy) and the resource allocations and spending decisions. It also identifies the challenges that need to be overcome in order for the budget to become a credible tool for allocating resources, in accordance with good governance.

Link between National Priorities and Public Expenditure

The Iraq National Development Plan 2010–14[1] was developed in 2009 amidst a difficult political and economic environment. The political and security situation was unstable and the outlook unclear, the volatility of oil prices caused at least three iterations of the NDP before a final price of between US$60 and US$68 per barrel was adopted, and a lack of data made it difficult to define baselines, which are needed for a meaningful monitoring and evaluation.

The NDP sets out the following seven main objectives: (i) increase gross domestic product (GDP) growth rate to 9.38 percent per year during the plan period;[2] (ii) generate 3–4.5 million new jobs; (iii) diversify the Iraqi economy away from oil and into agriculture (animal production, dates and fruits, and fisheries), industrial sectors (oil and gas, petrochemical industries, chemical fertilizers, cement, pharmaceutical industries), and tourism (recreational, religious, and historical); (iv) strengthen the role of the private sector, in terms of both investment and creating job opportunities; (v) reduce poverty rates by 30 percent from the 2007 levels by focusing on comprehensive rural development, job creation, and provision of basic services such as education and healthcare services, particularly for vulnerable groups such as youth and women; (vi) pursue sustainable development that balances economic, social, and environmental considerations, thereby optimizing the use of available natural resources without undermining the rights of future generations to benefit from those resources; and (vii) strengthen the role of local governments in developing their provinces, including through capacity building, and strengthening coordination and complementarities.

To achieve these objectives, the NDP proposes a total investment program of ID218 trillion (or US$186 billion) over the plan period, of which US$100 billion would be funded by the federal budget and the remaining US$86 billion would be funded by the private sector.[3] Sectorally, the NDP accords investment priorities to oil, electricity, agriculture, transportation and communication, and regional development (table 3.1). Higher investment priorities are given to the

Table 3.1 Allocation of NDP Investments, by Sector/Region

Sector/region	Percentage of capital investment
Agricultural sector	9.5
Oil	15
Electricity	10
Conversion industries	5
Transportation and communications sector	9
Construction and services sector	17
Education sector	5
Regional development	12.5
Kurdish Regional Government	17

Source: NDP.
Note: NDP = National Development Plan.

oil (15 percent of total proposed investment) and electricity (10 percent) sectors because they are seen as primary resources for development. Agriculture is seen as important from the perspective of economic diversification, food security, generating employment opportunities, and reducing poverty and migration to urban areas. The transportation and communications sectors are deemed critical in terms of enhancing connectivity with other sectors. The Plan reserves 12.5 percent of its investments for the regional development program, and 17 percent of total government investment, or higher depending on the next population census, to the Kurdish Regional Government (KRG). Finally, the plan allocates 22 percent of the government investment program to the social sectors (water and sanitation, health, education, sports, tourism, and cultural activities).

The NDP recognizes that investment alone is not sufficient, and proposes complementary policy and institutional reforms, and mechanisms for monitoring and evaluating the NDP. In terms of policy reforms, the NDP sets out the following fiscal policy reforms: reducing budget deficits, diversifying non-oil revenues, establishing a generations fund (sovereign wealth fund), improving budget preparation, reforming subsidies, and introducing responsible and effective management of internal and external debt. In terms of institutional reforms, the plan emphasizes the need for building human and technical capabilities; good governance based on the principles of rule of law, accountability, transparency, justice, and inclusivity; modernizing the public sector in accordance with these principles; use of modern technology; and verifying the cost-effectiveness of projects.

Another objective of the NDP is to establish a spatial development trend, characterized by fair distribution of infrastructure services and public services among all of Iraq's provinces, in a manner consistent with their population size and the extent of their deprivation and need. Despite these good intentions, the current administrative structures in Iraq reflect a strong centralist approach to governance, where administrative decentralization has not been meaningfully delivered, while subnational ministry structures continue as outposted departments of various central ministries. Box 3.1 summarizes shortcomings of the current system and suggests a way forward, based on previous work that had been done on fiscal decentralization and intergovernmental fiscal transfers in Iraq.

Box 3.1 Fiscal Decentralization and Intergovernmental Fiscal Transfers in Iraq

The Iraq Constitution lays the foundation for decentralized governance and the NDP calls for strengthening decentralized administration. The 2008 "Law of Governorates not Incorporated into a Region," while providing an initial platform for local governance, falls short in terms of offering specific guidance toward the establishment of an effective and efficient decentralized system. A key shortcoming of the law is that it devolves responsibility for the strategic direction and associated planning instruments to governorate councils, and it stipulates that budget allocations from the central government will support strategic plans, but it does not give governorate councils any leverage to influence the planning and resource allocation of line ministries through which the vast majority of services are provided. Technical departments that provide basic services such as water, electricity, health, and sanitation continue to receive their directives and budget allocations from their respective ministries in Baghdad.

At the governorate level, uncertain status and sometimes-competing administrations have resulted in inefficient administration across all sectors: This applies to essential services, socioeconomic development, security, and balanced representation.

Fiscal transfers: The 2010 budget introduced the notion of an absolute reimbursement of US$1 per barrel of oil to resource producing regions. This transfer mechanism intends to compensate these regions for special environmental and infrastructural costs. The adequacy of these amounts still needs to be assessed. At the same time, the 2010 budget introduced derivation-based revenue sharing for customs and in-bound airports of 5 percent, which may increase the incentives for subnational officials to encourage collections. Highly volatile revenues, such as those from oil, are best shared on the basis of a formula unlinked to derivation.

A way forward: Iraq will benefit from preparing a "decentralization policy paper," addressing inter alia; administrative organization and structure at the central, regional, provincial, and local levels; roles and responsibility of each level; resource allocations and mobilization; and related institutional development and capacity building. This policy paper would be informed by a comprehensive stocktaking of existing laws, regulations, and practices, and would be produced through a consultative process with stakeholders.

Source: NDP, Iraq Briefing Note, and Iraq Fiscal Decentralization Note.

Iraq Poverty Reduction Strategy 2010–14 and Targets for Reforms and Investment

The poverty reduction strategy, adopted in January 2009, complements the NDP by focusing on poverty. The NDP and PRS are linked in that they share a common goal of reducing poverty by 30 percent, from 23 percent in 2009 to 16 percent in 2014, through higher incomes and better health, education, social protection, and housing services for the poor.

Furthermore, the PRS sets out specific goals in terms of human development: (i) reduce illiteracy rate by half (from 28 percent to 14 percent), and raise net enrollment rate in primary (from 74.8 percent to 98 percent), intermediate (from 20.5 percent to 50 percent), and secondary education (from 23.4 percent to 40 percent); (ii) reduce the number of individuals covered by the food ration card and restrict coverage to those who are below the poverty line by 2014; and (iii) bridge the gender gap, including through higher women participation in the labor force, and higher ratios of girls to boys in literacy, and in primary and secondary education.

The implementation of the strategy envisages a combination of reforms and investment, namely: (i) better targeting and merging of the food ration and social protection systems; (ii) creating opportunities in rural areas that augment income, education, and infrastructure for the poor; and (iii) improving labor market opportunities for the poor. The strategy recognizes the need for effective monitoring and evaluation. and proposes to improve strategy-related databases in the relevant ministries and undertake household and statistical surveys to facilitate such monitoring and evaluation.

How Well Is Fiscal Policy Linked with the Strategic Priorities Identified in the NDP and PRS?

While Iraq has made considerable efforts toward producing comprehensive development plans, implementation has been slow. The NDP envisages the need to reorient spending from recurrent to capital spending, but that goal remains far from achieved. The NDP acknowledges that Iraq's spending policy between 2004 and 2008 sacrificed economic growth for temporary consumption. This is clearly evidenced by a noticeable increase in recurrent expenditures, in particular for employee compensations, social benefits (which include the public distribution system, social safety net), and subsidies to state-owned agencies and companies. In response, the plan sought to change the trend in the spending policy during the years 2010–14, and to do so in a manner that supports higher investment spending as a percentage of total public spending, while also controlling operating expenses and consumption. However, as the expenditure composition by economic analysis shows, that goal is yet to be achieved.

While the NDP emphasized the capital investment needed to achieve the goals, it pays little or no attention to the need to achieve efficiency and effectiveness for all public expenditure, including recurrent spending. Furthermore, with the adoption of the NDP and PRS, the translation of those national priorities would imply that spending composition would gradually change in favor of the social sectors, infrastructure, and regional development over the medium to long term. As the expenditure composition analysis by function shows, this again is far from being achieved.

Indeed, national priorities have not been sufficiently linked to the budget. One of the key challenges Iraq faces is aligning fiscal policy with the strategic priorities and objectives set out in the NDP and PRS. The NDP acknowledges that the capacity to direct public spending in accordance with the priorities and development objectives has been very weak. While there has been some progress in addressing budget preparation and planning issues through the PFMAP, the challenge of linking policy priorities with medium-term budgeting remains. For example, the 2010 Budget Strategy did not receive sufficient guidance from government. Priorities were developed and articulated after the strategy, and before the budget was finalized.[4] The 2011 budget was criticized in a number of dimensions, in particular for the weak medium-term context. It had a short-term view in terms of spending oil revenues as oil prices were increasing. More work is required from the government side to process emerging spending plans during the budget year. In 2011, new requirements for the recurrent budget came into picture during the discussion on purchase of F-16 aircrafts, increasing electricity subsidies, police and teacher salaries, and additional allocations to the ration card.

In practice, the budget formulation is dominated by ad hoc budgeting[5] and procyclical government spending, with little or no medium-term fiscal planning. The ad hoc nature of budgeting is manifested, among other things, in the practice of supplementary budgeting. This undermines the credibility of Iraq's budget formulation process, as the original budget is not adhered to. While a medium-term fiscal framework (MTFF) has been adopted, continued efforts are needed to introduce a credible medium-term fiscal framework that anchors fiscal policy to key policy documents such as the NDP and PRS, and which is based on sound economic and fiscal forecasts to bolster fiscal discipline. The Iraqi authorities will need support in these areas going forward.

The weak and ineffective budget preparation process results in budget submissions from ministries that are not in line with strategic priorities, unaffordable, and, ultimately, incapable of being implemented.[6] In 2009, the Council of Ministers Secretariat (CoMSec) suggested a timetable and process for the integration of the National Policy Framework into the 2010 Budget.[7] Appendix E summarizes the Iraqi budget process. The CoMSec timetable and Financial Management Law clearly show how priorities should be integrated into budget cycle; however, much more needs to be done if the budget process is to effectively link policies and resources. Appendix F shows how strategic planning process should work and how national priorities should feed into the budget process.[8]

The current challenge for the Iraq Budget Strategy Committee is how to best reflect the priorities in the 2013–15 Budget Strategy.[9] One approach implemented by the Budget Strategy Committee for the last budget strategy round was to form a smaller revenue forecasting, expenditure, and budget balance group. This proved to be an effective way of facilitating a managed discussion on the aggregate expenditure envelope, and should be followed again for 2013–15.

Proposed Work for Linking Policy with Budget

It is essential to link policy making with planning and budgeting to improve budgetary outcomes in Iraq. The Bank can help the Iraqi government to base policy framework of key spending areas on key policy documents, such as the poverty reduction strategy and the National Development Plan. Public expenditure composition issues could be assessed by a policy note, to see if fiscal decisions have been consistent with the national priorities. The Bank can help review the government's efforts to develop a medium-term fiscal framework and provide parallel training on macro and fiscal modeling. This will be a complementary effort to the work being implemented under the ongoing Public Financial Management Reform Project.

Commitment Devices

Once a reasonably formulated budget is in place, the government will need mechanisms to ensure that the expenditure path can be realized as envisaged. There will be two main challenges to this objective. First, the inevitable volatility in oil revenues will put cash flow pressure on the public expenditure management system, unless the latter has been appropriately insulated from the former. Second, there will be ex post pressures on budget implementation—as with any policy featuring winners and losers—to deviate from the agreed path. The general solution to this problem is to build the credibility of fiscal institutions so that there is acceptance (if only grudging) among politicians and the general public that the budget deviations would come at a high collective cost. In particular, it should be understood that, once the perception takes hold that various contingencies or pressures can lead to a revisiting of budget allocations, the "common pool" problem of revenues (that is, a race for a share of a pie that everyone owns) will be unleashed.

The most basic approach is to delimit the amount of revenue that is available for spending by the government. In the current political economy of Iraq, the propensity to consume out of "available" oil revenues will be extremely high: the case for allocating revenues to either capital or recurrent purposes will seem compelling. For this reason, oil exporters such as in Gulf Cooperation Council (GCC) use a reference oil price for the budget that is well below the spot or futures level of the price. For example, in Saudi Arabia and Qatar for 2012, the budget reference oil price is in the mid-US$60s per barrel. Although this is a fairly blunt instrument, it could be rationalized as a forecast that incorporates a precautionary component that discounts the central projection from its (mathematical) expected value.

Since the reference price is picked to be sufficiently low that the "surprise" will be on the upside, the bigger issue is what happens as revenues materialize ahead of the budget projection. While in principle the intent may have been to save all of the additional revenues, in practice supplemental budgets are inevitable. Ideally, supplemental budgets would be subject to the same processes—including legislative scrutiny—as the regular budget. One pragmatic way to impose some discipline on a supplemental budget is to have prepared a list of priority projects and funding requests during the time of the annual budget, with those closest to being funded during the annual budget forming a reserve list that gets included in the supplemental budget if additional revenues warrant it. In practice, however, supplemental budgets risk reacting to the pressures of the day midway through the budget cycle, at the expense of circumventing the normal budgetary

processes. The key point is that if the cautious reference oil price is not accompanied by a credible framework for handling the associated excess revenues, its
fiscal impact is likely to be limited.

The low reference oil price will also sit uneasily with other sensible budget reforms.
For example, a medium-term fiscal framework would be a useful way of framing
the link between the budget and the National Development Plan and poverty
reduction strategy, as discussed in the previous section. However, a MTFF would
be designed to produce a growth and revenue outlook to guide multiyear budget
formulation. If this process does not begin with a good-quality forecast of the oil
price, it is unlikely that it can model the overall macroeconomic outlook
correctly.

*Because of the pitfalls associated with using the reference oil price as an instru-
ment, a more formal fiscal rule may be needed.* The global experience with fiscal
rules is extensive, but translating this to the context of Iraq is not straightforward.
For example, fiscal rules are often formulated in terms of budget deficits and
public debt. Oil exporters are more likely to be characterized by budget surpluses, which correspond to extraction of a finite resource, necessitating an
approach based on wealth above and below the ground, and focused on how
large a surplus is necessary to ensure sustainability. Regarding a debt rule, Iraq still
lacks basic prerequisites for such a rule, namely consensus numbers on its overall
debt stock and clarity about the resolution of outstanding disputed debts.

One fairly direct approach to a fiscal rule would recognize that the current
postconflict environment results in having an unusually low level of GDP but
high growth in revenues, so *it may be useful to set a medium-term benchmark for
total public expenditure as a share of GDP.* A short-term benchmark is unlikely to
be useful because the spending share is currently inflated due to reconstruction
and political fragility. It is more realistic to expect that in 3–5 years, GDP will be
closer to its equilibrium path, and some of the immediate pressures for high
spending will have dissipated. However, in the short term, given that fluctuations
in nominal GDP are very much driven by changes in oil production and prices,
this fiscal rule might not be feasible. Rather, it is advised to continue, at least for
the coming years, with the practice of setting a relatively low reference price. In
the (likely) event that revenues would be higher, the government could then
decide to increase capital spending in the following year's budget. The experience
of other middle-income countries indicates that governments can meet a substantial range of functions with spending shares to GDP of around 35–40 percent.

Any fiscal rule will need to take into account the volatility of oil revenues. The volatility constrains economic planning in two ways: coping with departures between
actual and expected revenue given expenditure commitments, and the transmission of disturbances to the non-oil economy. Regarding the first problem, the
general principle is to decouple expenditures from cash flow shocks; once the
spending path has been determined according to a satisfactory rule, implementation should continue as the actual path of revenues is realized. The alternative—a
stop-start cycle in public spending—is highly disruptive. The implication of this
principle is that the path of spending will be smoother than the path of revenues,

meaning that some kind of buffer arrangement for revenue fluctuations is required. The purpose of this arrangement is to ensure credibility of the expenditure path in the face of revenue volatility, and in particular to have a framework for leaving expenditure plans untouched despite "normal" revenue variation.

The insulation of spending from revenue fluctuations is closely linked to impact on the non-oil economy of that volatility. As Gelb and Grasmann (2010) explain, one aspect of the often mediocre growth record associated with resource windfalls is the asymmetry in response of the non-oil economy to public spending; high levels of spending generate rapidly diminishing efficiency gains due to absorption constraints, but spending cuts can cause steep output and productivity declines, especially when they are implemented in an abrupt and across-the-board fashion. For this reason, a high propensity to save windfalls can be beneficial even if the revenue stream is fairly persistent, because deferred spending now can be somewhat caught up later, while commitments made now would complicate the adjustment to adverse revenue shock, with long-term growth consequences. Thus, while a standard future generations fund is a politically difficult proposition for Iraq, some kind of stabilization fund seems warranted. The choice of a fiscal rule is closely linked to the design of the fund: the government is picking a path for spending and a means of ensuring that the spending (and implied saving) path can be implemented.

How should the case be made that some spending should be deferred in the face of the constraints that Iraq faces ? Of particular importance is that the political system internalizes the adjustment costs that an overly rapid spending program will encounter. Unfortunately, incentives are usually in the opposite direction, as a scaled-up spending program is particularly susceptible to rent seeking, including from within the bureaucracy. Nonetheless, spending discipline will have to come from within the system. Ideally, the budgetary oversight mechanisms will be equipped with information to support a real-time value-for-money focus, such as frequent reports and analysis from the Board of Supreme Audit. Even basic information on spending disbursements by month or quarter could signal to parliament that there is a rapid expenditure flow, requiring enhanced scrutiny. A high frequency index of construction or engineering costs could also serve as a useful indicator in this regard, with policymaker alerts for spikes in the costs of key inputs.

Every commitment device will involve some role for a saving mechanism to decouple revenue from spending in the short to medium term. Although there is considerable experience worldwide with special funds designated for future generations or for expenditure smoothing, the lessons for Iraq from this experience are mixed. One underlying challenge is that the funds are rarely immune from the political pressures that they are intended to combat. For example, even if a fund has a clear future generation mandate (meaning that it can't be used to finance spending), its asset allocation strategy may come into the political arena. The fund may be pressed to invest domestically or to backstop guarantees issued to domestic entities; the most damaging scenario is when the fund is directly used to finance off-budget spending. Although difficult to quantify, there is also a risk that the presence of a fund induces moral hazard, as policy-makers come to view the fund as insurance against events or trends that they would otherwise seek to mitigate. Once the fund comes into play in this fashion, the principle of having it walled off from the general budget is undermined. For this reason, it may be more effective to have explicit ground rules linking the fund to the budget from the start, and the recent trend has been to better integrate funds with budget systems.

While a stylized future generations fund is not yet appropriate for Iraq, some mechanism for smoothing in the short to medium term seems warranted. One simple version would take the form of a stabilization fund, where budget surpluses can be allocated to finance budget deficits. However, these funds could have more elaborate saving and withdrawal policies. Specifically, as proposed in the Country Economic Memorandum (CEM), the facility could be a "parking fund" where oil revenues are accumulated while the public expenditure management system is at its most constrained, and then gradually released to finance spending needs as absorptive capacity improves.

Regardless of the type of fund used, it is important to note that as things stand, the Development Fund for Iraq does not currently serve these purposes. The Development Fund for Iraq (DFI) provides an assurance that Iraq's oil revenues are not being dissipated at the stage between customer payment and receipt by the government. Thus, it is a revenue custodian rather than a savings fund. In addition, for reasons of macroeconomic management, it is useful for the government to house oil revenues off-shore such to avoid disrupting the day-to-day market for foreign exchange, but in itself this does not correspond to any fiscal goal. Once transferred to the budget, revenues are subject to all the risks inherent in a weak public expenditure management system.

Fiscal rules present shortcomings in Iraq, weakening further the fiscal discipline. The major examples are virement practice and off-budget spending. The authorities need to curtail the use of within-year spending reallocations to ensure parliamentary oversight and compliance with the budgeted expenditure composition. In the context of changing expenditure priorities throughout the year, the Ministry of Finance frequently resorts to reallocating appropriations, without parliamentary oversight, of the current budget to address shifting needs. It is unclear whether these changes in the allocations are recorded in the final trial balances submitted for Board of Supreme Audit (BSA) and Council of Representatives (CoR) review. It is important to note, however, that the Ministry of Finance (MoF)'s shifting of funds is explicitly authorized in the budget laws passed by parliament, which is in contradiction with the public financial management law. The text of the budget laws includes sections that create ambiguity in the budget tables that are attached to the law. Thus, the actual composition of spending does not reflect the budgeted composition of spending presented in the budget tables approved by the parliament.

The authorities need to end their reliance on off-budget spending, and fully recognize loans taken from banks Rasheed and Rafidain to finance state-owned enterprise (SOE) salaries. In 2011, the authorities spent approximately ID 9 trillion without proper budgetary allocations via advances, and rolled over more than ID 2 trillion in unused investment budget allocations from 2010. Some of this off-budget spending was financed via loans from banks Rasheed and Rafidain. The authorities have accumulated about ID 12 trillion in this type of loans; none of which are reflected in the government balance sheet, or recognized by the MoF's debt directorate. The transfers to SOEs financed via off-budget loans are known in advance by the MoF's budget department, but are not included in the following year's budget. In addition, the off-budget spending is not reflected in the monthly trial balances nor in the budget documents submitted to the BSA or CoR.

Public Investment Framework

A related issue is the absence of an effective Public Investment Management Framework in Iraq. This is required to strengthen the capacity to implement infrastructure projects. The importance of public investment management comes from the need to have in place the infrastructure to deliver essential public services like health, education, water, and electricity. All these services require capital investments, which is problematic for Iraq.

The prime minister has identified key priorities in the government's program for 2011–14 with a vision to improve the capacity of the oil sector, production of oil and gas, transport infrastructure, and the provision of electricity, while also improving services. The key priorities are as follows: (i) promote the production of oil, gas, and petrochemicals: enhance the ability to produce and refine oil and gas flows through the rehabilitation of existing refineries and the creation of new ones; These would be developed and implemented through investment contracts with international companies, and would encourage investment in petrochemical industries; (ii) increase the storage capacity of oil and gas and develop the transport network; (iii) improve the distribution of oil and gas to Iraqi citizens; (iv) improve the quality of petroleum products and gas according to international specifications; and (v) promote the shipping industry and its facilities. The prime minister also identified improving the transport networks as a key area. The government's action plan is to rehabilitate various means of transportation, with rural areas given special attention. Another important target is improving the provision of electricity without interruption, through improving the performance of power plants to meet the growing demand for electricity. The government plans to rehabilitate power generation plants and distribution. The development and expansion in this area will lead to the introduction of renewable energy. The government will take all possible measures to rationalize the consumption of electricity.

There is, however, a lack of medium-term perspective and well-costed sector strategies to support these objectives. Spending decisions do not have clear links to sector strategies and cost implications are not well reflected in the MoF's set of internal forward budget estimates, though linkages to indicative budget ceilings are improving. While basic sector strategies have been prepared for some departments, an agency or sector strategy has not been developed sufficiently to enable proper costing on a medium-term consolidated and resource constrained basis.

Some ministries lack investment planning. The 2010 BSA Report found that the Ministry of Construction and Housing did not have a work plan for 2008 to follow up investment implementation projects by the ministry's entities for infrastructure rebuilding projects, such as roads, bridges, and houses. In addition, the ministry did not have an investment budget database, and the Follow-up and Planning Departments did not have projects' updates. The ministry requested the information from its entities only when they were asked to provide it.

As a result, they rely excessively on subcontractors, who may not be impartial, or technically and financially reliable enough, for detailed design and implementation. The BSA found that some of the contractors hired by the Ministry of Construction and Housing had no experience in construction work. Most companies recorded losses and had low levels of projects' technical implementation despite the contracts' period extension. The contractors relied on the advanced payments to implement the projects.

Furthermore, it is unclear how much exactly gets invested as investment budget, and accounting remains opaque. The Ministry of Planning (MoP) and the MoF appear to be well aware of the systemic factors that are constraining cash-based investment budget credibility. In particular, the continuing use of 100 percent letters of credit (LC) for project contracts is constraining the cash-based appropriation system for investment budgets.[10] Appendix G reveals that within the investment budget the size of uncleared net advances (of which letters of credit is a subset of suspense accounts) and hard commitments (net creditors) is significant. The use of delayed payment contract arrangements is further fragmenting the budget and making it more opaque. Moreover, the fact that investment budgets do not split planned allocations by economic type of expenditure is another major source of opaqueness. Data available to date have not been sufficient to make better and more informed assessment of investment budget. Further work will be required in this area. In the meantime, accelerating progress toward a unified budgeting, accounting, auditing, and appropriation control framework remains critical. In this regard, classification, accounting, and auditing standards will need to be agreed by MoF, MoP, and BSA as a matter of priority.

Worse, the budget framework is unstable, as the virement process allows for within the year reallocation. This is done in a nontransparent manner, as is often the case with recurrent spending. Budget allocations can be adjusted throughout the year based on spending unit budget performance, with a correcting revised appropriation table provided to the CoR with the following year's budget. Investment and recurrent budget planning remains fragmented, with recurrent and administrative costs of investments not properly accounted for.

Unsurprisingly, Parliament has criticized the 2012 infrastructure budget. The Economic and Investment Committee has objected to the allocation of infrastructure projects within the 2012 budget, claiming that not enough detail has been given. The committee announced that the latest budget does not include enough information on spending—with the exception of the US$2 billion allocated for housing. The government has allocated US$15 billion (ID 17.3 trillion) for infrastructure projects in the 2012 budget. The committee highlighted that the government must show spending allocations and priorities in detail to inform the Council of Representatives about the infrastructure budget, adding that the Council of Representatives cannot agree on the financial allocations without such information.

Execution of the Investment Budget

As already noted, there is a chronic underexecution of the capital budget. From 2005 to 2010, on average only 57 percent of what had been planned was executed.[11] Investment budget execution performance worsened in 2011. Table 3.2 compares investment budget allocations and execution rates by selected ministries and governorates between September 2010 and 2011. The table shows that budget execution rates were already low in 2010 for key investment sectors, such as oil, electricity, public works, health, education, and water resources. Additionally, performance worsened for majority of these sectors in 2011.

The 2010 BSA Statement reported that despite serious infrastructure deficiencies the investment budget was not executed efficiently. For example, investment budget allocations for the Baghdad Municipality were not fully executed in 2008. Further, budget execution rates for the overall investment budget were 11 percent, regions development was 24 percent, and emergency plan was 6 percent. Most Baghdad areas do not have any sewage services, as the existing sewage system is from the 1960s and uses expired concrete pipes. Sewage and rainwater systems open on each other, and both drain into the Tigris directly, which increases pollution levels. Main sewage lines are overloaded and backed up due to the aging of the sewage pumping stations, and the stations inability to keep up with the population increase.

A number of factors affect execution rates of capital budget. These range from security restrictions to weak project approval processes, procurement, and contract management issues, to administrative capacity. For example, both the Ministry of Electricity and Ministry of Oil struggle with weakness in capacity and ineffective budget process. Procurement practice is weak and nontransparent in both sectors. Despite some positive developments, such as finalizing an integrated national energy strategy, the strategic planning is still not appropriately translated into budget allocation and execution process.

The problem starts at the commitment stage. Iraqi law requires full funding for a project to be contracted out, even if this a multiyear project, thereby limiting the number of project starts that can be made in any year. This is despite the fact that budget projections show these projects can be afforded. For example, in the electricity sector, the ministry faces difficulties in funding of generation projects due to the Iraqi budgetary system. In response to these issues, the ministry has attempted to commence a number of projects on a deferred payment basis; however, it is struggling to find contractors willing to accept such terms.

Republic of Iraq Public Expenditure Review • http://dx.doi.org/10.1596/978-1-4648-0294-2

Table 3.2 Comparison of Investment Budget Allocations, Actual Spending, and Execution Rates, by Selected Ministries, September 2010 and September 2011

ID million, unless otherwise indicated

Ministry	September 30, 2010 Revised investment budget allocations	September 30, 2010 Actual spending	September 30, 2010 Budget exec. rate (%)	September 30, 2011 Revised investment budget allocations	September 30, 2011 Actual spending	September 30, 2011 Budget exec. rate (%)	Change in alloc. (%)
Oil	3,103,550.000	1,584,478.0	51.1	7,142,182.389	2,029,792.000	28.40	130.1
Electricity	4,173,503.000	3,627,946.0	86.9	3,953,479.700	2,826,662.400	71.50	-5.3
Defense	278,190.000	100,411.0	36.1	262,581.041	43,520.334	16.57	-5.6
Interior	312,200.000	50,689.0	16.2	199,755.280	50,126.000	25.09	-36.0
Reconstruction and Housing	750,411.825	383,687.0	51.1	1,059,189.500	343,055.600	32.39	41.1
Science and Technology	37,039.544	5,315.0	14.3	47,197.481	10,401.712	22.04	27.4
Municipalities and Public Works	1,531,476.000	1,008,517.0	65.9	1,578,831.000	558,984.000	35.40	3.1
Labor and Social Affairs	24,711.900	8,853.0	35.8	27,886.000	8,902.000	31.92	12.8
Higher Education and Scientific Research	408,961.969	91,954.0	22.5	612,313.908	151,827.500	24.80	49.7
Youth and Sport	550,000.000	255,900.0	46.5	896,743.525	258,944.600	28.88	63.0
Education	503,897.765	28,584.0	5.7	644,555.904	161,582.500	25.07	27.9
Trade	91,438.000	2,449.09	26.8	112,108.531	14,549.000	12.98	22.6
Planning	66,526.485	20,602.0	31.0	50,843.700	2,953.825	5.81	-23.6
Industry and Minerals	921,024.297	560,674.0	60.9	1,343,867.915	976,842.440	72.69	45.9
Health	1,127,000.000	152,661.0	13.5	1,060,000.000	119,767.000	11.30	-5.9
Water Resources	1,139,718.964	418,510.0	36.7	1,705,620.578	678,196.000	39.76	49.7
Agriculture	207,674.834	65,505.0	31.5	351,948.300	49,279.000	14.00	69.5
Transport	537,167.287	101,692.0	18.9	577,388.465	233,160.000	40.38	7.5
Communications	394,034.500	112,386.0	28.5	470,090.000	57,366.000	12.20	19.3
Office of the Prime Minister	192,400.000	151,208.0	78.6	123,682.535	26,288.000	21.25	-35.7
Kurdish Regional Government	3,438,448.404	2,565,889.0	74.6	4,354,964.253	2,811,144.000	64.55	26.7
Baghdad Municipality	788,952.000	472,000.0	59.8	878,507.021	275,000.000	31.30	11.4
Total	25,157,534.117	13,246,108.0	52.7	35,247,582.405	13,853,897.110	39.30	40.1

Source: Republic of Iraq Ministry of Planning, Government Investment Program Department (September 2011). Investment Budget and Actual Expenditure.

The solution to the problem is utilizing one of, or a combination of, two approaches:(i) a fully functional medium-term accrual of a cash based top-down and bottom-up fiscal framework, which forces authorities to enter into multiyear contracts that are limited to a parliament-endorsed set of detailed estimates that are properly maintained and scrutinized; or (ii) an obligation system of appropriations, where authority to spend is provided over a fixed multiyear period, but is fully supported by a system of accounting controls and reporting systems (covering both cash, apportionments, and obligations). At the moment, Iraq has neither system.

Procurement procedures are weak in implementation, particularly when contractors are also involved in project planning. While the reform of the legislative framework for procurement is progressing,[12] implementation is slow. For example, reliance remains on uncompetitive procurement methods; incomplete, unreliable, and untimely procurement information for the public; a nonoperational independent administrative procurement complaints system; and inadequate inventory control. In Iraq, the use of open competition for the award of contracts is limited and the extent of justification for use of less competitive procurement methods is alarming.[13]

Passing a procurement law in line with World Bank recommendations would help attract much needed investment in infrastructure. The authorities do not have a clear framework for contracting and financing large-scale infrastructure projects. This lack of framework leads to a lack of interest by big international firms to embark in projects in Iraq, unless the Iraqi authorities pay for the costs upfront. Since most of the infrastructure that Iraq needs to build would require multiyear expenditure, and would require a long life span, these projects would be accompanied by long-term financing. Iraq does not have a clear framework for project selection, and does not have the legal authority to pay for multiyear projects across several fiscal years via project financing without parliamentary approval. Thus, some ministries have resorted to signing multiyear contracts with creative financing schemes without proper vetting by the MoF and MoP. In 2011, for example, the Ministry of Electricity signed multibillion dollar deals for electricity generation using the so-called "deferred-payment" method, under which the government would pay for the cost of the project and an implicit financing charge upon project completion, without parliamentary approval. It was later found that one of the contracting companies was bankrupt and that the other did not exist.

Weak commitment controls increase the risk that cash and appropriations are not well managed. This can lead to pressures including unnecessary formal and informal sequestrations and virements over funding of investment projects. This can also result in disbursement delays at national and subnational levels. The MoP is responsible for tracking commitments of projects in the investment budget. Commitment control is currently limited to the system for approval of contracts and availability of appropriated cash. Hard (signed contracts) and soft commitments (required allocations for agreed projects and programs) are not systematically tracked, making it difficult to plan disbursements well.[14] The Public

Financial Management (PFM) Project is developing a "Cash Management and Commitment Control Framework" that will be implemented under an Integrated Financial Management Information System (IFMIS). This would complement the Public Expenditure Review (PER) by contributing to improving the efficiency of public expenditure.

There are also constraints with letters of credit. The BSA reported from the audit result that there are expired letters of credit that were not processed in the Ministry of Oil accounts, and pending LCs from previous years that still show on the companies' records. The 2011 Ministry of Planning report on "Problems and Obstacles of Implementing Investment Projects" called attention to the long process time associated with opening LCs for importing goods, machines, and necessary equipment to implement investment projects. Appendix I presents a flow chart showing that it takes 39 days to process LC issuance, 49 days for LC payment, and 47 days for clearance of letters of credit. Also, the same document highlighted that opening LCs is limited to the Trade Bank of Iraq, with a complex mechanism based on having approval from the Ministry of Finance and Ministry of Planning.

However, the reported underexecution is not only an outcome of inefficiencies, but is also due to the different "reporting systems" of the MoP and MoF. While the reports of the MoF are based on cash-based accounting system, the reports of the MoP are based on accruals. The MoF reports the budget execution only after there has been a cash release from the consolidated fund, and after it has been adjusted for in their relevant chart of accounts. The MoP, on the other hand, includes letters of credits and advances issued to vendors in their reports on budget execution.

The Case for Public Investment Management Framework in Iraq

The importance of public investment management issues derive from the need to have in place the infrastructure to deliver essential public services like health, education, water, and electricity. All these services require capital investments like hospitals, clinics, and schools. The past few years in Iraq have seen persistent underspending of the government's capital budget, although there are recent signs that the situation may be improving slowly.

One of the most significant challenges facing the Government of Iraq is to improve the integration of capital and recurrent budgeting (PEFA 2008). This common problem in PFM results from insufficient attention being paid to the recurrent costs of capital schemes and therefore significant difficulties in operating and maintaining expensive capital assets. Institutional arrangements are found to be important, with responsibilities for different aspects of budgeting being divided between the MoF and the MoP. In Iraq, these difficulties are enhanced by large parts of the investment budget being financed and executed outside the budget by donors.

Other issues identified in the recent PEFA (2008) were weak capital investment planning, resulting from limited capacity to develop sector strategies; project feasibility studies; credible project costing and realistic project appraisals;

continuing lack of consistency and uniformity in budget documentation and classification; bottlenecks at every stage of the process, from procurement and contract management through to commitment; verification and payment to oversight; poor coordination between implementing ministries and inadequate delegated authority; and market imperfections including the unstable security situation, supply bottlenecks, fuel shortages, private sector constraints, and difficulties in resolving land disputes.

This PER proposes to provide an institutional assessment of the public investment management system in Iraq following the diagnostic framework developed by Rajaram, Minh Le, Biletska, and Brumby (August 2010), which has identified the critical features that an effective public investment management system must have to improve the quality of spending.[15] These include: (i) investment guidance, project development, and preliminary screening; (ii) formal project appraisal; (iii) independent review of appraisal; (iv) project selection and budgeting; (v) project implementation; (vi) project adjustment; (vii) facility operation; and (viii) project evaluation. Each of these features (Figure 3.1) will be examined in the context of Iraq. Additionally, the challenges Iraq faces in each area will be highlighted and recommendations will be provided on the priority reforms that Iraq would have to implement to bring its public investment management system in line with recognized standards of efficiency and transparency in managing public investment. An issue that will receive particular attention is the need to better identify operations and maintenance (O&M) cost implications in budgeting for new and ongoing projects and to assess the adequacy of budget allocations for the rehabilitation of existing infrastructure. This work could be done in collaboration with the ongoing PFM Reform Project. Under the PFM project, the team is currently providing support to Ministry of Planning in strengthening investment project preparation and appraisal through following set of activities: (i) review and modernize, as needed, provisions and procedures for the preparation and appraisal of large projects; and (ii) set criteria for appraising medium-size and small projects. In addition, control and audit functions will be part of institutional needs assessment.

Public Investment Programs (PIPs) are considered to have been a cornerstone of national policies of governments which consider the improvement of their infrastructure as a springboard for economic growth. Recent literature on Public Investment Management (PIM) concur that governments in developing and transition countries in normal times devote more public resources to infrastructure initiatives than governments in developed countries. In times of crisis, governments are forced to impose drastic cuts to capital expenditures, often forcing the cancellation or postponement of planned infrastructure projects. In both situations, it is imperative to have an effective PIM system in place to maximize value for money.

However, these trends are not always matched by efforts to improve Iraq's PIM. PIM theories call for a stagewise reconsideration of the entire investment project cycle, while at the same time an overhaul of the related institutional changes; Iraq is no exception. Authorities now consider it imperative to enhance the quality and efficiency of PIM. One way to do this is to move away from administrative compliance toward performance management of public investment, while another way is to improve the preparation and economic rationale of the proposed projects. In the literature on capital budgeting and project evaluation, a growing consensus is consolidating around the necessity to "put the management in charge" to render as flexible as possible the project response to the unforeseen changes in a world where uncertainty dominates.

Spending through the PIP in Iraq is expected to grow in the coming years. The Ministry of Planning foresees significant increases in public investment, particularly in the oil and electricity sectors. The 2011 budget aimed to accelerate investment in public services and in oil infrastructure, as well as to accommodate additional social safety net and security outlays. Iraq's rehabilitation needs remain large, particularly the improvement of public service delivery and the rebuilding of essential infrastructures, which are critical to help create a private sector that can provide sufficient employment opportunities to the country's large labor force. The government is keen on accelerating the pace of investment, while recognizing the constraints posed by the limited implementation capacity. Large investment outlays are also envisaged for the oil sector, including payments to the international oil companies for recovery of their costs and investments. The MoP prioritizes the following sectors: drinking water and sewage projects, housing projects, school and hospital construction projects, transport and irrigation projects, land reclamation projects, electricity projects, and extractive industry projects.[16]

Advancing the PFM reform program will be essential to execute public investment efficiently and effectively. A sound and effective PFM system, with well-established

Figure 3.1 Important Features of a PIM System

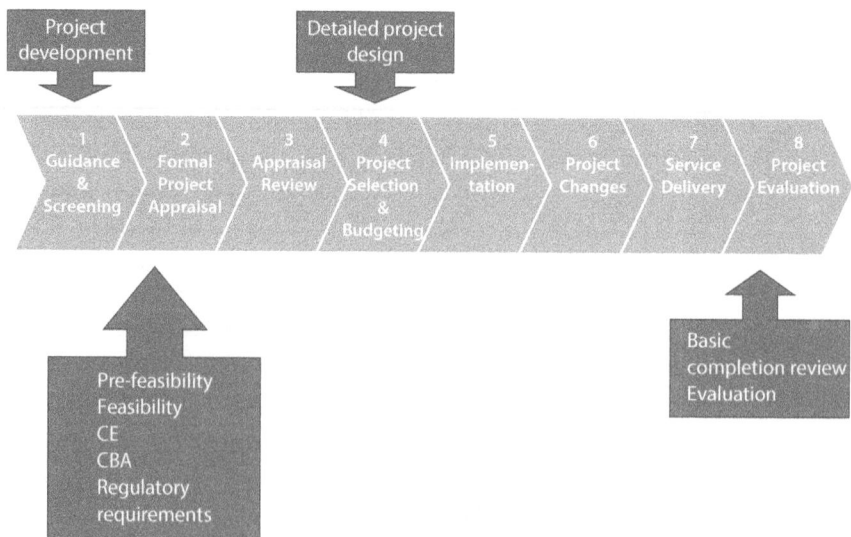

rules and procedures for the preparation, execution, and reporting of the budget, will increase the prospects of achieving key economic and social objectives, support accountability and transparency, and prevent leakages of public resources. Iraq has made notable progress in reforming its PFM system. It has established a sound legal framework to manage its public finances and the computerized expenditure management system will help to improve transparency. However, significant challenges remain. Enforcement of the new procurement rules and regulations has been weak, and capacity to implement procurement in a timely and transparent manner remains limited.

Conclusions and Recommendations

This chapter discussed strategic planning and budget execution issues, in order to have the greatest impact consistent with good and well-articulated government policy. It highlighted the need align national development planning and the poverty reduction strategy, to help decide resource allocation, and also highlighted the importance of fiscal rules that bring the discipline required for medium-term policies to be followed. The final two sections stressed the need for a credible public investment management framework with strong institutions, systems, and business processes.

The next two chapters illustrate the points made above in the context of two sectors: electricity and health. Both sectors suffer from fiscal discipline, strategic prioritization, and operational efficiency issues, as discussed in this report.

Notes

1. The plan is available at: http://www.iauiraq.org/documents/1159/ndp24th.pdf.

2. In the oil and gas sector, the NDP plans to increase the quantity of exported crude oil from its level of 1.894 million barrels per day in 2008 to approximately 3.1 million barrels per day in 2014. In addition, the plan aims to increase dry gas production (from 800 million square feet per day in 2008 to about 2,200 million square feet per day in 2014), and refining capacity (from 0.580 million barrels per day to about 1.450 million barrels per day by 2016), and reduce burned gas (from 700 million square feet per day in 2008 to 150 million square feet per day).

3. The NDP spells out the relative roles of the private and public sectors and states: "the private sector plays a leadership role in creating wealth and jobs, while the public sector plays an organizational and enabling role to address market failures, guarantee fair distribution of the national income, and see that at-risk social groups can effectively fulfill their role in achieving economic and social progress."

4. Adam Smith International (2011). Discussion Paper: 2012–14 Budget Strategy. Department for International Development.

5. The NDP laments the historical practice of line-item incremental budgeting as having been the source of many budget rigidities in Iraq, and contributing to the lack of strategic orientation of the budget.

6. World Bank (September 2011). Iraq Governance Policy Note: "Addressing Governance Challenges in the Short and Long Term."

7. Adam Smith International (2009). Discussion Paper No. 3: *Linking Priorities and Resources, 2010*. Department for International Development.

8. Adam Smith International (2010). Discussion Paper: 2011 Budget Strategy. Department for International Development.

9. World Bank (2012). Discussion Paper: 2013–15 Budget Strategy.

10. If this remains due to the private sector being unwilling to accept purchase orders (contractual/promises to pay), it raises particular issues with arrangements proposed for delayed payment contracts.

11. There have also been wide divergences in budget execution rates between ministries and governorates. Only the relatively stable and more secure region of KRG has been able to achieve a high level of budget implementation.

12. A draft Procurement Law was prepared in 2008 and submitted to the Council of Ministers for approval subsequent to its review by the Shura Council in December 2009. However, the Committee of Economic Affairs of Council of Ministers decided in its session of October 6, 2011, to go ahead with the preparation of public procurement regulations now and consider preparation of law at a later stage. Currently, a committee led by the Prime Minister's legal advisor had been established to prepare draft regulations that would incorporate the main elements of the draft Law. The World Bank continues its support to public procurement through (i) strengthening and supporting Iraqi public sector procurement system; (ii) institutional capacity building and strengthening of key Iraqi regulatory authorities at the Ministry of Planning (the Government Contracting Directorate), implementing and controlling institutions, and private sector organizations in public procurement; (iii) assisting with public procurement, procedures, documents, and practices; (iv) addressing governance issues including complaints mechanism relating to procurement; and (v) assisting the Iraq BSA to improve its control and audit practices on procurement. The support to BSA on improvement of procurement practices was provided through two initiatives: procurement audit training by the International Labour Organization (ILO) and a procurement audit peer review by the French Court of Accounts, both jointly coordinated by the World Bank.

13. World Bank (2008). Public Expenditure and Institutional Assessment Volumes I and II, Washington DC.

14. Adam Smith International (2011). Technical Working Paper: Iraq—Fiduciary and Development Risk Assessment. Department for International Development and Swedish International Development Cooperation Agency.

15. Rajaram Anand, Tuan Minh Le, Nataliya Biletska, and Jim Brumby, "A Diagnostic Framework for Assessing Public Investment Management," Policy Research Working Paper WPS 5397, World Bank, Washington, DC, 2010.

16. Investment Budget and Actual Expenditure (September 30, 2011). Department of Government Investment Programs, Ministry of Planning, Iraq.

CHAPTER 4

Case Study #1: Electricity

Introduction

The challenges facing efficient service delivery in Iraq's electricity sector can be summarized as follows: low electricity supply performance and serious shortages; ambitious investment plans (especially for generation); low cost recovery, with a significant fiscal burden on public budget; and limited management capacity for investment prioritization. Electricity supply is inadequate to meet demand, and there is a chronic shortage, despite recent efforts to increase electricity supply. The damaged transmission and distribution networks, combined with the lack of generating capacity, makes it difficult to meet current demand. A combination of low tariffs, excessive losses, and expensive imports result in high operational expenditures. The sector heavily relies on government funding, given that the cost of power vastly exceeds revenues. There are serious deficiencies in public service delivery because of the weak capacity to implement infrastructure projects.

This chapter focuses on these electricity sector-related issues and their implications to Iraq's economic and social development in terms of fiscal discipline, investment prioritization, and sustainable service delivery. There is an urgent need to address these issues, which would require (i) efficient management of investment programs (generation, transmission, distribution, and fuel feedstock supply); (ii) improvement of collection rates; (iii) rationalization of tariff structure for financial self-sustainability (or at least reducing the financial burden); and (iv) regulatory and institutional reform. Followed by a sector overview, this chapter analyzes the fiscal issues and proposes further work to increase the efficiency of service delivery.

Sector Overview

Iraq is among the countries best endowed with energy resources. Currently, the energy sector (oil, gas, and power) is Iraq's most significant economic sector. The sector has suffered during almost three decades of conflict and political turmoil, which has left its institutions weakened and has resulted in underinvestment and chronic deterioration in energy infrastructure. The energy sector continues to face serious issues, including chronic shortages of electricity supply, an inability to supply natural gas as fuel for power generation, and increased levels of associated gas flaring. Therefore, new policy initiatives and investments are required in order to improve the efficiency and potential of the energy sector. A coordinated investment policy in the electricity sector would be a key part of the country's recovery strategy.

Electricity supply is inadequate to meet demand, which is seen by Iraqis today as a top concern. In addition to negative impact on Iraqi households, inadequate and poor electricity services and infrastructure impede private sector development. Power shortages are estimated to cost the Iraqi economy around US$40 billion per year.[1] Despite some recent improvements, electricity supply continues to fall well below demand, with a national average of only around eight hours per day of electricity supply and a supply deficit of 39 percent in 2010.[2] The current supply situation is exacerbated by deteriorated network conditions due to many years without appropriate new investment, which has left all three components of the system—generation, transmission, and distribution—in a significantly degraded condition. The physical and operating conditions of the existing power generation stations are such that many units need massive rehabilitation or replacement. New generating units (mainly gas turbines) have been installed, but their operation often suffers because of fuel supply problems, especially the lack of infrastructure to provide natural gas, which is the preferred fuel for this type of generating unit and which is currently being flared in significant quantities associated with Iraq's oil production. The transmission and distribution networks were damaged during the conflicts in 1990s and 2000s and have been negatively affected by chronic deterioration, deliberate destruction, and sabotage. As a result, some parts of the network are heavily loaded and are subject to repeated interruptions. This situation, combined with the lack of generating capacity, makes it impossible to meet the current demand.

The electricity sector is regulated and managed by the Ministry of Electricity (MoE). The MoE is vertically integrated to manage the operational functions (power generation, transmission, load dispatch, and distribution) and their assets, except for Kurdish Regional Government (KRG). Functionally, the MoE has responsibility and authority for policy setting, regulations, planning, engineering and projects, and operation and maintenance of electrical assets. The MoE is also responsible for suggesting tariffs levels, which must be approved by Council of Ministers. The KRG MoE has a similar structure, and manages the assets located in the KRG. There is no grid connectivity between the federal network and the KRG network—essentially the KRG operates a separate islanded system. In other words, both ministries ensure parallel operations, with limited integration, covering separate geographic regions. In order to establish a closer coordination and improve operational efficiency and adequacy of regulations, a new Electricity Law (approved by the Council of Ministers and currently under review of the Council of Representatives) mandates that the MoE oversees all activities in the electricity sector in Iraq, including in the KRG. Looking forward, reforming the state institutions in charge of the electricity sector will be necessary to establish efficient public service delivery and rebuild government credibility.

The challenges that Iraq faces in the electricity sector are not only physical in nature; they are also financial, economic, legal, regulatory, and more significantly institutional, including a lack of capacity. These challenges are hampering effective strategic management of the sector, as well as fiscal sustainability, planning, development, and operation of its physical infrastructure. Electricity tariffs remain nominal, and are far below the level of cost recovery—it is estimated that tariff revenue is collected only on around one-third of the electricity that enters the distribution network,[3] and thus makes no contribution to capital costs. The transmission and distribution (T&D) losses are much higher than internationally accepted levels, at around 35 percent[4] of the electricity consumed in 2010 (compared to around 17 percent in Turkey and 15 percent in Jordan). The electricity sector therefore remains highly subsidized. In addition to these systemic issues, there is a weak interministerial coordination between the MoE and the sector stakeholders such as the Ministry of Oil, Ministry of Finance, and the Ministry of Planning & Development Cooperation, complicating efficient functioning of the electricity system. Adequate operational relations among these authorities would require strong legal and regulatory reforms. The lack of capacity, particularly in the Ministry of Electricity, for project preparation and implementation affects investment performance and public investment budget execution for electricity. Each year, the Ministries of Electricity of Iraq and KRG submit their investment and operational budget allocation requests in accordance with the ceiling set by the Ministry of Finance for the electricity sector. However, the budget execution for electricity by the line ministries remains low.

Given the economic and institutional challenges, the Government of Iraq has initiated several studies to provide a solid analytical background for decision makers. In this regard, the Ministry of Electricity first completed in December 2010 an Electricity Master Plan for Iraq, with assistance from the U.S. Government. A separate master plan was developed in 2009 for the KRG. These plans produced forecasts for capital investment requirements on generation, transmission, and distribution sectors. In addition, the Integrated National Energy Strategy Technical Assistance (INESTA) Project, funded by the World Bank Iraq Trust Fund, has been initiated to create an Integrated National Energy Strategy (INES) for Iraq. INESTA's vision is to develop the energy sector in a coherent, sustainable, and environment-friendly manner, to meet domestic energy needs, foster the growth of a diversified national economy, improve the standard of living of Iraqi citizens, create employment, and position Iraq as a major player in regional and global energy markets. The INES is a comprehensive strategy for the overall energy sector, with the main emphasis on the short and medium term. It provides a framework for energy policies and investments, and highlights investment priorities.

Status of the Electricity Sector

There are more than 3.5 million customers in Iraq, including the KRG. Households represent about 82 percent of these customers, consuming about half of the billed electricity. Industry and commerce, representing 15 percent of the number of customers, consume about 25 percent of the sold electricity. Most of the large industrial customers are mainly concentrated in the north and south of Iraq. In geographical terms, about 23 percent of electricity is consumed in the Baghdad area and 21 percent in the KRG.[5] The electricity demand forecasts expect a shift toward the industrial segment in long term. Residential and commercial demand is projected to grow at the same rate as the overall economy. Despite long period of conflicts, the access rate in Iraq is good, at 98 percent.[6]

Demand for Electricity

The electricity peak demand[7] in Iraq is estimated at 13.7 gigawatts, and has increased significantly over the past five years, showing an average annual growth rate of around 9 percent. The consumption of electricity (sales) in 2010 was 8.3 gigawatts, meaning that only 61 percent of demand has been satisfied with existing supply, including imports. According to different scenarios, electricity peak demand is expected to reach a level between 22 gigawatts (with a 5 percent increase per annum) and 27 gigawatts (with a 7 percent increase per annum) by 2020.[8] This could mean more unserved customers if the investments in power sector (generation, transmission, and distribution) do not pursue a strong and coordinated path of growth. The balance between supply and demand first depends on additional available generation capacity, but transmission and

Figure 4.1 Billed Energy Breakdown, by Consumer Type
TWh

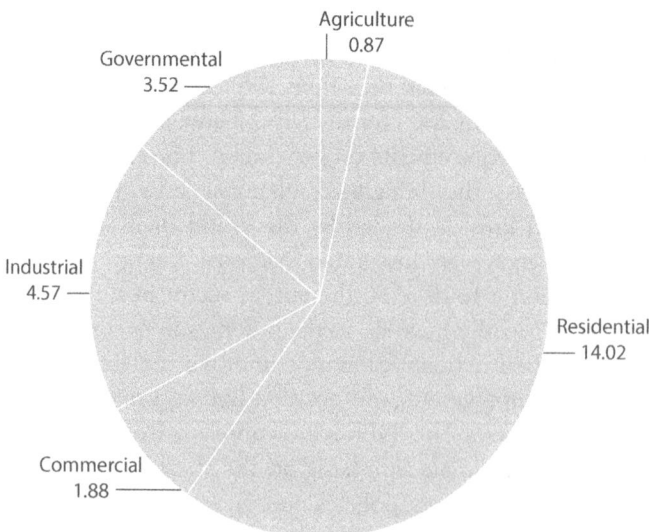

Source: Iraq and KRG Electricity Master Plans, December 2010.

Figure 4.2 Demand and Supply Balance, 2006–20
base case, GW

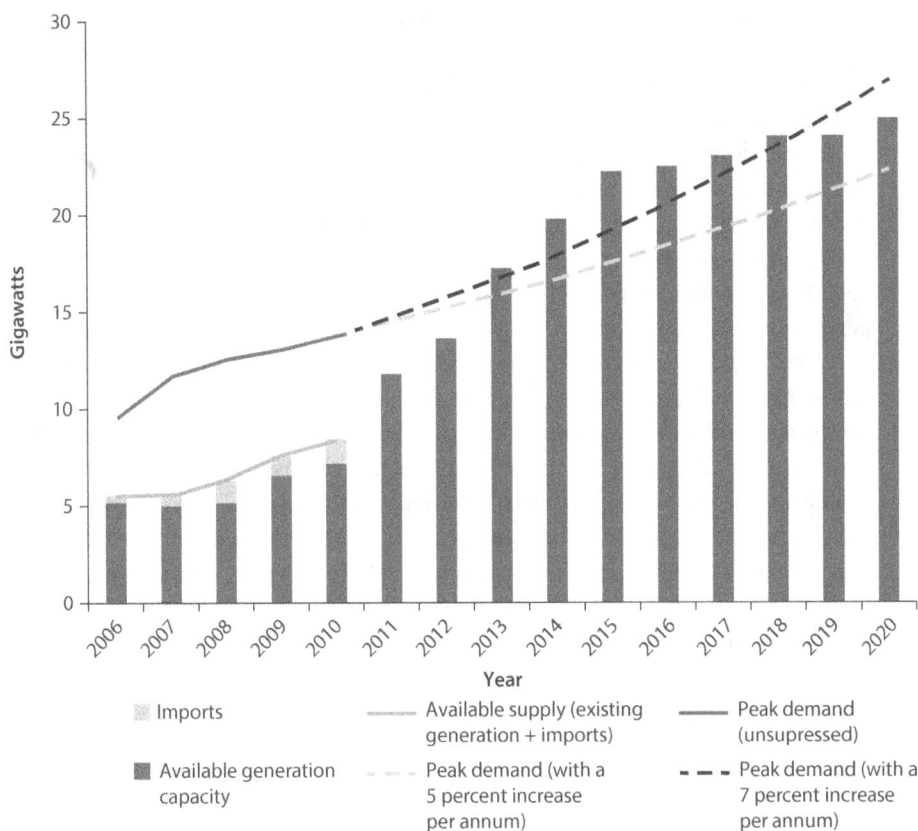

Source: International Energy Agency (IEA); and World Bank analysis based on "Integrated National Energy Strategy (INES)" Study, 2012.

distribution congestion may still influence the ability to satisfy future demand. There are measures that can reduce peak demand. The demand-side measures (creating energy efficiency standards, utilizing different types of tariffs for target customer segments, and developing awareness programs among major customer segments) could reduce peak load requirements by 10–15 percent through efficient sector management and prioritized investments. Developing a reliable power system in Iraq will require major investments in assets, operations, and management, especially in generation capacity.

Generation and Shortages in the Supply

Iraq possessed in the past a relatively robust electricity system. However, many years of sanctions, conflict, and lack of adequate investment have resulted in a system struggling to keep up with a rapidly rising demand. The people of Iraq are consequently suffering considerable shortages in electricity supply. The chronic shortage affects all governorates, limiting electricity supply to eight hours per day on average.[9] This shortage is caused by both inadequate generation and by transmission and distribution outages. Urban centers within each governorate typically have more supply hours. Electricity is a major economic driver, and shortages have a direct impact on productivity and outputs due to loss in production time, damage to products and capital assets, and increased output costs. The deteriorated transmission system and poor quality of the network are also severely impacting economic development. Many businesses have to invest a significant amount of their revenues in expensive private generators. The electricity shortages have an indirect impact through intersector linkages and spending, for example by limiting private sector development. The shortages also reduce the efficiency of public spending, causing expensive electricity production through short-term diesel generation, barged power, expensive power imports, and excessive losses.

Over the past years, Iraq's power generation system has deteriorated from one of the best in the Middle East region to a situation where power supply has become insufficient and extremely unreliable. Iraq has a nameplate installed generation capacity of 15.3 gigawatts. Capacity is distributed across the country at 47 different locations, of which 37 are simple cycle gas turbine (SCGT) power plants. The maximum technical achievable capacity is 12.3 gigawatts, and only 65 percent of this capacity (8.3 gigawatts) is practically available to serve existing demand. This is due to several reasons, such as non-ISO conditions (–3 gigawatts), aging (–1 gigawatts), and fuel and water and several outages (–3 gigawatts). This means that the present available generating capacity is capable of supplying only approximately half the peak demand, which is estimated to be 13.7 gigawatts.[10] *Existing generation capacity is more than 20 years old, and requires replacement over the next 10–20 years.* Thermal power plants face low availability due to frequent unplanned outages: the national average availability is about 68–70 percent for both gas and steam turbines. Another reason for this low availability is fuel shortage from shutdowns at oil refineries and gas processing facilities. Some level of fuel shortage persists throughout the entire year, due to the misalignment between fuel production, storage and consumption, and inadequate fuel transportation logistics. Correcting this imbalance will require not only increased gas supply but also improved connections to the gas pipeline network. This issue mainly affects power plants in the central regions of Iraq. Most large plants in the north and south of the country have relatively reliable access to the supply of piped gas from the northern and southern pipeline systems. For instance, to overcome the fuel-availability problem, the MoE signed a US$365 million contract under which the Islamic Republic of Iran would build a 140-mile-long pipeline to transport natural gas from the Islamic Republic of Iran to Baghdad, meeting fuel needs for Iraq's gas-fired power plants (especially the Qudas and al-Sadr power plants).[11] In the case of hydropower plants, the situation is similar. Hydropower plants have suffered water shortages due to drought, neglected water infrastructure, and diversion by upstream countries (the Syrian Arab Republic, the Islamic Republic of Iran, and Turkey). The whole hydro system is suffering from a lack of maintenance, and due to the climatic conditions of the region (low in-flows). Most hydro-dams were also designed primarily for irrigation. In addition, the country does not have a formal agreement specifying its water consumption quota with upstream countries. Reduced annual precipitation at source countries has diminished water flow in both the Tigris and Euphrates rivers.

New power generation capacity is of crucial importance, in addition to the continuing need for investments in transmission and distribution. The short-term plans (2009–15) mainly consist of (i) installing small gas turbines (<125 megawatts)[12] and small diesel engines (30 megawatts); (ii) rehabilitating and expanding existing plants; and (iii) building new steam and hydro plants. The target for available generation capacity by 2016 is 22 gigawatts. In this regard, the MoE has a committed plan for the installation of nearly 13 gigawatts of new generation. About 10 gigawatts of this generation will come from gas turbines, ordered through the Mega Deal contracts with General Electric and Siemens, with the remainder coming from steam turbines, diesels,[13] and a small hydro plant. According to the MoE's projections, this amount of committed capacity will help satisfy the unsuppressed demand by 2014. Between 2017 and 2022, it plans to build a flexible power generation capacity to use heavy fuel oil and gas for SCGT and combined cycle gas turbine (CCGT). Power capacity ramps up quickly in the short term to catch up with demand; in the longer term CC capacity is being added. Iraq currently does not have any CCGT plants. This increase in generation capacity will significantly address current shortfalls in demand, but will also test Iraq's transmission and distribution systems.

Figure 4.3 Cost of Electricity, by Technology, 2010

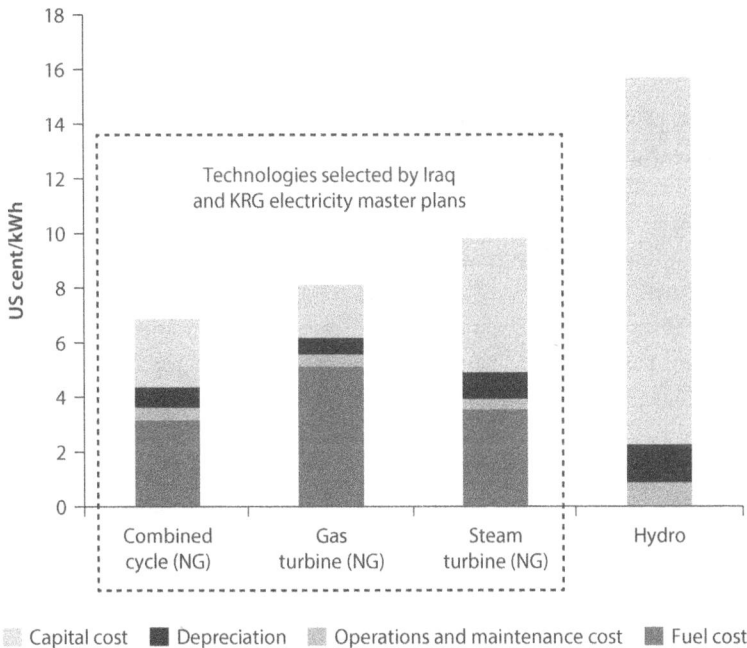

Source: INES Final Report 2012.
Note: KRG = Kurdish Regional Government.

The Ministries of Electricity of both the Central Government and the KRG have recently completed electricity sector master plans, which call for continued expansion of gas turbine generation. The Electricity Master Plans (both for Iraq and the KRG) have prioritized the combined cycle, gas turbine, and steam turbine plants, using natural gas as fuel of choice. This will place increased pressure on the need to rehabilitate and expand the badly deteriorated gas supply infrastructure. Iraq is believed to have significant untapped gas resources: proved reserves are 3.2 TCM (to compare; Norway: 2.0 TCM and Indonesia: 3.1 TCM, these two countries are also intensively commercializing their natural gas reserves) with annual production currently only at around 1.3 billion cubic meters (bcm)/year in 2010[14] (in comparison, Turkey's natural gas consumption was 40 bcm in 2010). Large quantities of associated natural gas are currently being flared because the gas treatment plants and the pipeline infrastructure are not functional. For instance, over 40 percent of the production in 2008 was flared, due to a lack of sufficient infrastructure to utilize it for consumption.[15] In Iraq, discussions focus on potential integrated natural gas projects throughout the southern fields, while the gas projects in the KRG are increasingly geared toward electricity generation. However, the flaring of associated gas remains a critical issue that will only be resolved by appropriate levels of investment in gas treatment and supply infrastructure.

The shortages in generation have forced the government and the public to find alternative short-term solutions, such as diesel generators and power import. Around 80 percent of the Iraqi population relies on diesel generators (DGs) for electricity supply as a primary and secondary source, due to a lack of available supply from the grid. These DGs (with a total estimated capacity of 8 gigawatts and 21 TWh, produced 30 percent of the total electricity in Iraq in 2009)[16] increase demand for gas oil, cause additional high cost to consumers, and produce negative environmental effects, such as noise and CO_2 pollution in major urban centers. The widespread use of private diesel generators is a major cause of poor air quality in cities. In addition to DGs, Iraq imported 6.7 TWh of electricity (16 percent of total consumption): 4.8 TWh from the Islamic Republic of Iran and 1.3 TWh from Turkey in 2010.[17] The Syrian interconnection has been inactive since 2005. According to the Ministry of Electricity, Iraq will stop importing electricity from neighboring countries once new units are introduced, and energy production will reach 20,000 megawatts. However, a 400 kilovolts transmission line[18] connecting the Islamic Republic of Iran and Iraq has been recently completed and will thus increase Iraq's reliance on electricity generated by the Islamic Republic of Iran.

Distribution and Transmission Issues

Eighty three percent of the power distributed in Iraq is unbilled or uncollected, causing significant revenue losses. The transmission and distribution (T&D) losses in Iraq are comparatively high, mainly due to technical issues, the prevalence of electricity theft, and meter tampering. The losses represented 43 percent of the energy produced in power generation systems in 2010 (the typical range of T&D losses is around 8–12 percent in the rest of the world). As a response to this issue, the MoE has planned to replace and refurbish aged transmission substations and

Table 4.1 Estimated Distribution of Investment, 2011–20

Distribution rehabilitation	2011–15
Number of existing BSPs	209
Cost per BSP (US$ million)	40.9
Total cost (US$ million)	8,548
Cost per year (US$ million)	1,710
Distribution from new BSPs	
Number of new BSPs	38
Cost per BSP (US$ million)	122.2
Total cost (US$ million)	4,644
Cost per year (US$ million)	929
Total cost (US$ million)	13,192
Total cost per year (US$ million)	2,639
Distribution rehabilitation	2016–20
Number of new BSPs	32
Cost per BSP (US$ million)	122.2
Total cost (US$ million)	3,910
Cost per year (US$ million)	782

Source: Iraq Electricity Master Plan, 2009–10.
Note: BSP = bulk supply point.

lines, and to expand the 400 kilovolts network to accommodate increased generation capacity. The MoE has also included (in its investment plans) programs to reduce commercial and technical losses in distribution, through expansion and strengthening of the distribution network in alignment with growth in electricity load. It also plans to address network bottlenecks. In addition to infrastructure investments, in the medium to long term, the ministry also needs to address the requirement for preventative and regular maintenance, combat electricity theft, improve meter reading, billing, and collection, and restructure tariffs.

Iraq's transmission network provides relatively good national coverage, compared to problematic generation and distribution components in the electricity system. However, bottlenecks and supply constraints still remain. The existing Iraqi transmission network serves all of the country's major population centers, and uses 400 kilovolts and 132 kilovolts transmission lines. The latter network is the local load distribution network within each governorate, with a few 132 kilovolts ties to neighboring governorates, while the 400 kilovolts network is the national grid bulk power transfer highway between the governorates and with neighboring countries.[19] Uncontrolled and unplanned expansion has resulted in the low-voltage (LV) distribution network being overloaded, however. Insufficient energy metering and tariff subsidies also have contributed to overloads. Pervasive connection of distributed private generation to the LV network results in reduced network reliability. Maintenance suffers from a shortage of spare parts and a lack of standardized practices. Recently, the MoE has been able to restore damaged transmission lines with minimal or no effect on the availability of supply on the national grid, due to the interconnectivity and redundancy in the Iraqi electrical system. The growth of high-voltage transmission lines and towers in Iraq has been slow, due to their particular vulnerability to disruptions and attack. These attacks take place mainly in central and northern Iraq. Therefore, the rehabilitation of the transmission and distribution networks has similarly been slowed by a combination of security concerns and budget constraints, and suffers from bottlenecks and overloading. Future demand growth requires extensive reinforcements, upgrading, and construction of additional transmission lines. According to the Electricity Master Plans, the investment needs are important, and are estimated at around US$4 billion for 132 kilovolts and 400 kilovolts reinforcement, including generation connections.

Considering the time frame for appropriate investment, there is good potential for renewable energies, especially solar for off-grid solutions. Iraq's renewable resource endowment is large, with the potential to supply 29,000 TWh/year, mostly from solar energy (concentrated solar power). This is quite significant when compared with other similar countries: 1,000 TWh in Spain and 6,000 TWh in Jordan, for example. This solar energy can be generated from an area that is 3 percent of the territory in Iraq, mainly in the southwestern part of the country. In the North, given the long lifetime of hydro assets and their multipurpose uses in tourism, irrigation, agriculture, and fisheries, hydropower is an attractive option for the KRG: its potential is estimated at 5 gigawatts (the KRG Electricity Master Plan identified eight hydro projects of 400 megawatts). However, effective exploitation of the region's hydro resources faces challenges such as requirement for

Figure 4.4 T&D Network Growth, 2009 and 2020

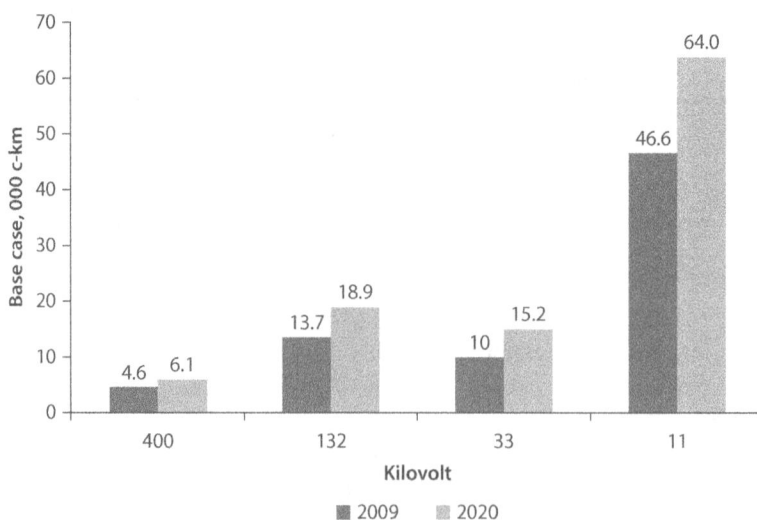

Source: Iraq Electricity Master Plan and INES Final Report, 2012.

long-term capital-intensive investments and expansion of transmission interconnectivity with major electricity demand centers in the rest of Iraq. As a whole, the renewables (concentrated solar power, photovoltaic, and wind) capacity could reach 1 percent of installed capacity by 2015 and 4 percent by 2030.[20]

Fiscal Issues

Tariff Structure

Iraq has an inefficient and weak tariff vs. cost recovery structure compared to other Middle East and North Africa region countries. Iraqis have little incentive to use electricity efficiently, due to the low cost of electricity through existing nominal tariffs, which are subsidized by the government. Bill payment is also poor due to the lack of efficient metering and efficient payment collection. The prevailing electricity tariff for final consumers is very low when compared to Middle East and North Africa region countries. The country has adopted a unified tariff structure across all customer segments: residential, commercial, governmental, and industrial, which is one of the lowest. In 2008, it was US$0.8 cents/kwh for the tariff range for consumption of 250–1,000 kWh per month in Iraq while it was 14.7 U.S. cents/kWh in Morocco and 12.5 U.S. cents/kWh in neighboring Jordan. Only 8–10 percent of the end user tariff (1 U.S. cent/kWh) covers the total cost of the electricity sold (11.8 U.S. cents/kWh).[21] Tariffs are based on an escalating consumption slab structure. However, the lowest slab width of 1 MWh is too wide to have a big impact on curbing residential consumption. Iraq currently does not have a seasonal electricity pricing. Activation of the new tariff structure proposed in April 2011 (Table 4.2) has been postponed due to opposition from several governorates and widespread dissatisfaction with service reliability.

Tariffs only cover less than 10 percent of fuel and operating costs.[22] Tariffs in a self-sustaining electricity sector cover operating expenses (OPEX), depreciation,

Table 4.2 Ministry of Electricity Tariffs, by Customer Type, 2008–11
U.S. cent per kWh

Consumption (kWh per month)	Jan. 2008 to Sep. 2010 All	As of Oct. 2010 Domestic, commercial, and governmental	As of Oct. 2010 Industrial and agricultural	Proposed as of April 2011 Domestic, commercial, and governmental	Proposed as of April 2011 Industrial	Proposed as of April 2011 Agricultural
1–1,000	0.83	1.66	10	0	0	0
1,001–2,000	1.66	4.16	10	4.16	10	4.16/10.00
2,001–3,000	2.5	6.66	10	6.66	10	4.16/10.01
3,001–4,000	2.5	8.33	10	8.33	10	4.16/10.02
4,001+	4.16	11.25	10	11.25	10	4.16/10.03

Source: U.S. Congress, Iraq Report 2011.

and the cost of capital, while regional oil-rich countries typically have tariffs that cover at least OPEX (including fuel) and some or all of the depreciation of assets. In Iraq, a combination of excessive losses and expensive imports result in OPEX that are 12 times the average end user tariff. For instance, if distribution losses were reduced from 40 percent to 5 percent, the total operating cost per unit of electricity would be 7 U.S. cent/kWh. Therefore, the power sector is heavily subsidized by the government.

Sector Efficiency

On the whole, service delivery efficiency in the sector is very low, and costs are high in terms of recurrent and capital expenditures and opportunity costs. The electricity sector subsidies represent a fiscal burden. Amounting to US$21 billion in 2010, subsidies accounted for 11 percent of the government OPEX and other recurrent expenditures, and the power plants received around US$2 billion subsidies. The implicit and explicit subsidies together amounted to 36 percent of crude oil export sales revenues in 2010.[23] To reduce this financial burden, the government needs to address the subsidy issue as a whole, and must rationalize its energy infrastructure, including power. In addition, the system's inefficiencies are reflected in the MoE's manpower levels (per full-time-equivalent "FTE"), which seem excessive in relation to its system size compared with other countries in the region.

The electricity sector is facing major supply and efficiency issues, and should consider new approaches and solutions, such as more independent power producer projects. In the medium-/long term, independent power producer (IPP) project financing offers significant benefits, such as leveraging management capacity, bringing additional financing, and technology transfer. Iraq plans to have 40–50 percent of its power generation coming from IPPs by 2030.[24] So far, the MoE has called for private investors to participate in four power stations, with a total capacity of 2.5 gigawatts, but has failed to attract feasible proposals due to the obligation of using the gas turbines bought by the MoE, and due to the lack of an independent regulator. The MoE is currently working on a new approach to overcome these issues. The short-term potential solutions, such as using oil as collateral, encouraging the international oil companies to fund the power plants near their fields, and ship excess power the MoE grid, could be used to face capacity issues for new power generation. In addition, a new institutional and regulatory framework will be needed to develop sustainable IPP investment schemes. The KRG has established an IPP track record in capitalizing on recent development of its natural gas resources. The IPPs in KRG are gas-fired simple cycle gas turbines (with a capacity of 625 megawatts) that are supplied via a pipeline from the Khor Mor gas field. The KRG MoE plans to maximize private sector involvement. The IPP revenue requirement payments are guaranteed through an advanced payment account with a third-party financial institution. However, IPPs have some limits in the short-term, for example inadequate fuel supplies currently limit the promotion of new IPP schemes. IPPs also rely on diesel as a secondary fuel if gas is not available. The quality of diesel required by

Figure 4.5 Generation, Transmission, and Distribution Sector Productivity, 2009

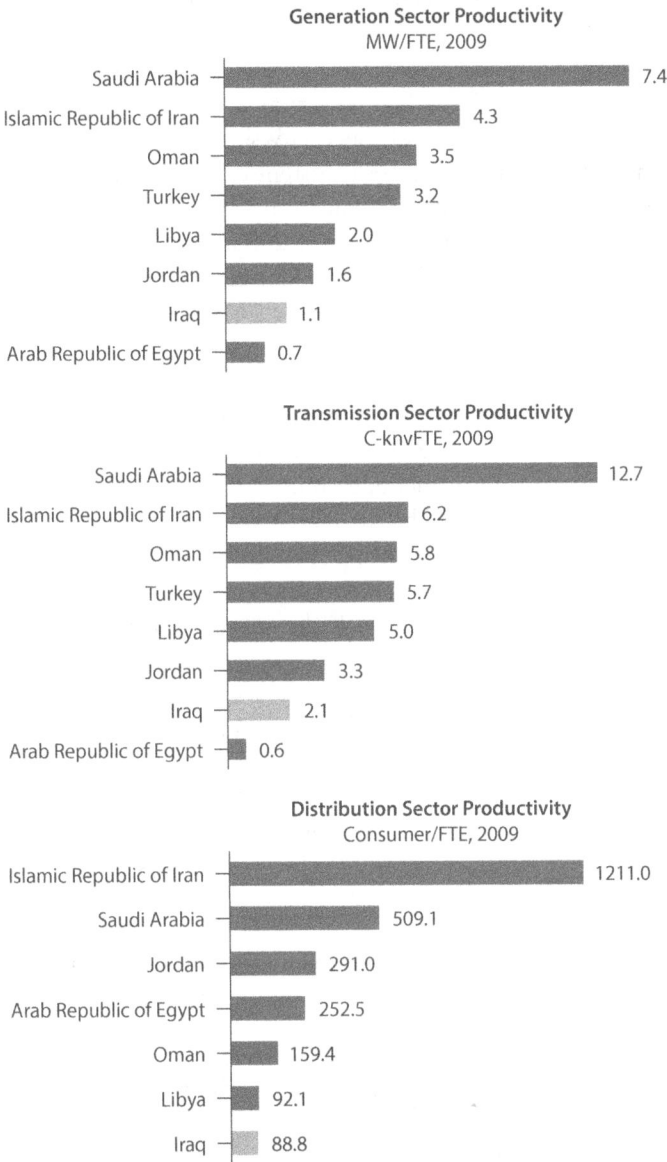

Generation Sector Productivity
MW/FTE, 2009

Saudi Arabia	7.4
Islamic Republic of Iran	4.3
Oman	3.5
Turkey	3.2
Libya	2.0
Jordan	1.6
Iraq	1.1
Arab Republic of Egypt	0.7

Transmission Sector Productivity
C-knvFTE, 2009

Saudi Arabia	12.7
Islamic Republic of Iran	6.2
Oman	5.8
Turkey	5.7
Libya	5.0
Jordan	3.3
Iraq	2.1
Arab Republic of Egypt	0.6

Distribution Sector Productivity
Consumer/FTE, 2009

Islamic Republic of Iran	1211.0
Saudi Arabia	509.1
Jordan	291.0
Arab Republic of Egypt	252.5
Oman	159.4
Libya	92.1
Iraq	88.8

Source: INESTA Final Report, 2012.

the IPP contracts cannot be covered by domestic Iraqi production for the time being, and so has to be imported from Turkey or the Islamic Republic of Iran.

Investments in the Electricity Sector

The challenges analyzed in the previous sections require prioritized and efficient investment strategies. The ongoing reconstruction efforts have direct implications for public finances in the light of large-scale expenditure needs. The development of coordinated policy and strategy in the energy sector is a key part of the country's recovery strategy. The overall cost of the development of the electricity sector is very large, but the economic benefits will pay back the investment many times over.

In total, the electricity expansion program will require US$83 billion of capital expenditures over the period 2011–30. The Government of Iraq (GoI) has allocated US$22.7 billion to the Ministry of Electricity since 2006. Forty two percent of this funding has been used to cover recurrent expenditures, mostly salaries. Additional funding worth US$5.3 billion from the U.S. Government has been used for 550 energy-related projects since 2003. The GoI has awarded several major contracts to international companies for generation capacity development projects. The contracts have been funded by a US$4.8 billion increase in the Ministry of Electricity's budget allocation for capital expenditure between 2009 and 2010. Should these and other ongoing projects be completed by 2015, 12,000 megawatts will be added to Iraq's supply. By that time, it is estimated that demand will have increased to about 21,000 megawatts, meaning that Iraq may still face a shortfall in supply. Implementing committed plans requires US$30 billion, of which US$13 billion would be for short-term generation. This results in a high investment need of US$6 billion per year from 2011 to 2015. In the long term, the required investments will average about US$3.5 billion per year.

Significant public expenditures and efficient budget execution will be required in the early years to bridge the supply-demand gap. The government investments cover generation assets as well as the rehabilitation and expansion of the transmission and distribution networks. Most of the funding will come from the government, as IPPs will require more mature financing and legal frameworks. The investment level tempers down as supply and demand are met beyond 2015/16 and the bulk of upgrades to the transmission and distribution network are completed.

Figure 4.6 Public Investment Budget and Oil versus Electricity Investment Spending, 2005–10

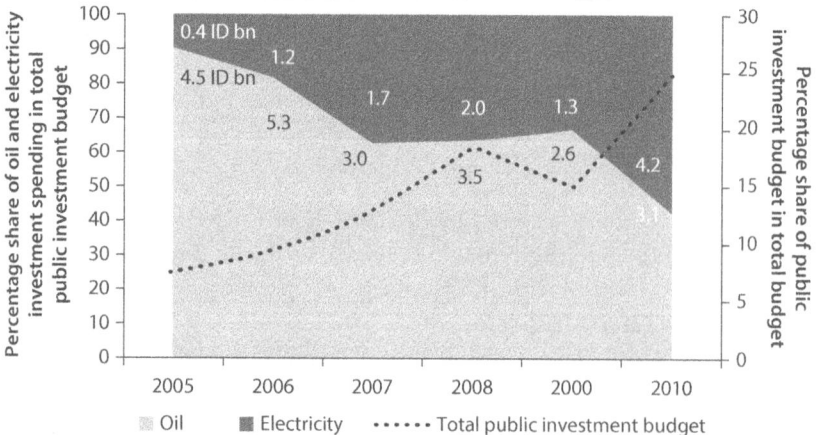

Figure 4.7 Investment Needs for Energy Sector, 2011–18
US$ billion

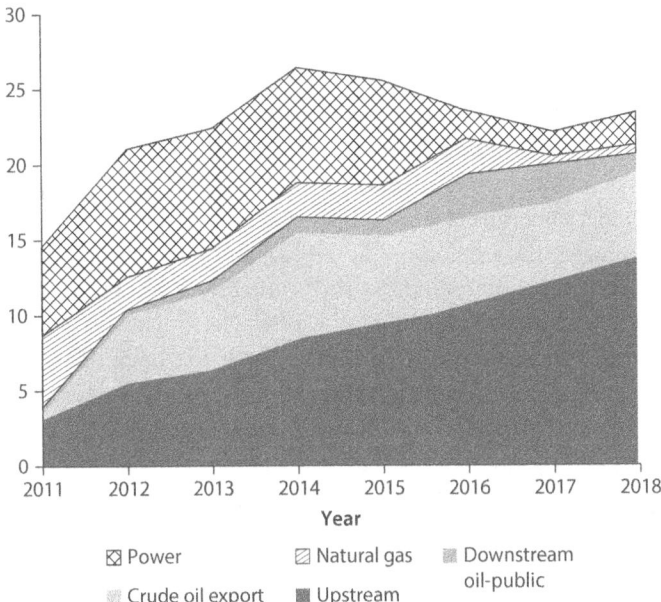

Sources: Iraq Energy Master Plans 2009–10; and INES Final Report, 2012.

Figure 4.8 Recurrent and Investment Budget Execution in Electricity Sector, 2005–09

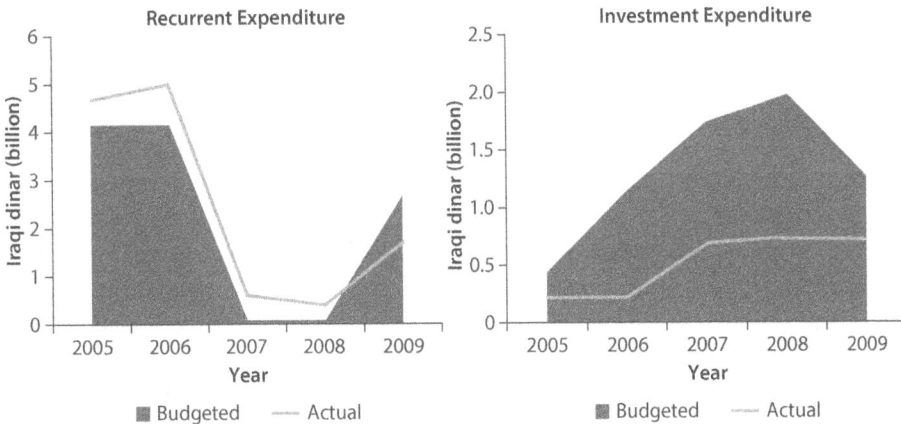

The public investments suffer from a low budget execution rate, attributable to heavy bureaucracy, a slow procurement process, and a lack of institutional capacity. Currently, government policy for public investments has been moving in the direction of emphasis on rapid growth in recurrent spending, while much of the capital budget was being managed through a deficient procurement and contracting system. It seems that there has been some improvement in project preparation support at the Ministry of Planning, especially in terms of the quality of submissions from the governorate level, which are now more likely to feature reasonable quality feasibility studies.

Regulation and Institutions

A number of legal and institutional priorities need to be addressed for efficient sector coordination in Iraq. At institutional level, separating policy making, regulations, and operations from the MoE should be the first step in implementing any reform agendas. The establishment of a Holding Company or an Electricity Commission with an independent regulator is to be planned to allow corporatization of the MoE, and privatization and public-private partnership potential in the electricity sector are being considered. At the regulatory level, the current efforts to develop new regulatory codes for new pricing mechanisms should continue, so that electricity prices increase to at least cover the operating costs. To address the urgent need to increase generation capacity and attract IPPs, the authorities are recommended to consider transitory regulatory paths, including regulation by contract.

The MoEs of the Federal Government and KRG are organized along the value chain, with functions executed centrally. However, there is a degree of repetition between central and regional functions on power production, transmission, and distribution. The generation and transmission operations are currently combined; their future separation is key in preparation for sector commercialization. There is a lack of focus on strategic support functions, such as the supply chain (contracting and procurement), and training and HR development. The country should develop a structured mechanism in coordination with the Ministries of Industry and Mining, and should develop the capacity expansion plans necessary to attract investment. A national policy of electricity tariffs, including clear responsibilities for federal, regional, and private entities, is to be developed and implemented. In the long-term, a national strategy for electricity market reform should take into consideration options for the commercialization of the MoE entities, unbundling of operational sectors, and different forms of private sector participation.

In projecting needs and executing investments, the MoE needs greater coordination with several governmental entities. The MoE interfaces with several key government stakeholders (Ministry of Finance, Ministry of Oil, Ministry of Planning and Development Cooperation, Ministry of Industry & Minerals, Ministry of Water Resources, and KRG MoE) to predict demand, manage fuel supply, and obtain funding. The misalignment of schedules for maintenance and purchases limits operational efficiency and causes serious supply bottlenecks and shortages of key liquid fuels. For instance, there is no formal fuel supply agreement between the MoE and Ministry of Oil (MoO), leading to a lack of clarity on detailed responsibilities (that is, for delivery of fuel from depot to power station). To address this issue, the MoE and the MoO jointly plan fuel requirements, an effort that exhibits many challenges. The Ministry of Oil, which allocates hydrocarbon reserves across Iraq, allocates fuel for power plants; however, there is no clear policy for hydrocarbon allocation to priority sectors, including power. The MoO also lacks a clear vision on long-term development plans and production levels for fuel oil and natural gas. This undermines capacity expansion planning, due to the lack of a clear outlook on fuel availability. The MoE consequently faces several interruptions in fuel supply.

A new law for restructuring the MoE is being issued as part of a revised legal framework for the sector. The draft electricity law has been approved by the Council of Ministers and is currently being reviewed by the Council of Representatives. The law establishes the Ministry of Electricity as the entity responsible for all operational activities in the electricity sector in Iraq, covering generation, transmission, and distribution. The law grants the MoE the right to develop overall sector strategic vision, goals, master plans, policies, and feasibility studies for expansion projects; grants licenses for private participation in electricity activities; and allows it to develop and enforce Health, Safety, and Environment (HSE) regulations. The law stipulates that state-owned entities (SOEs) under the supervision of the MoE will be self-funded. The law also gives the right to the MoE to propose tariff levels proportionate to operating expenses, after approval from the government (Council of Ministers [CoM] and Council of Representatives [CoR]). The law includes a provision to establish different consumption categories that include residential, commercial, industrial, government, and agricultural, and an authority to take disciplinary actions in case of delayed payments or theft (in the form of suspension of service or financial penalties). In addition, a regulatory law has been drafted, but will need the electricity law to be passed to become effective. In preparation, the MoE has taken steps to establish an embedded "regulatory office." The regulatory office is not an independent regulatory body, but a function within the organization of the Ministry of Electricity. The head of the regulatory office (Minister's Advisor for regulation) serves a consultative role. The minister retains key authorities including major appointments, approval of regulations and operating procedures, granting of generation licenses, and recommendation of tariffs to the Council of Ministers. The MoE has also launched efforts in drafting a number of licensing codes and technical regulations.

Conclusions

As discussed above, the issues in the electricity sector components (generation, transmission, distribution, and regulation) are widespread. Examples include aging infrastructure, shortages in fuel supply, low cost recovery, poor planning and budget execution, a lack of coordination among sector stakeholders, and shortages in funding. There are serious issues in delivering essential public services because of the weak capacity to implement infrastructure projects. Despite a large public sector in Iraq, the service delivery remains poor. The power sector offers one of the most notorious examples of serious deficiencies in public service delivery in Iraq. There has been a chronic gap between electricity supply and high demand, and the sector heavily relies on government funding, given that the cost of power vastly exceeds revenues. In the short to medium term,

rehabilitation of the electricity sector is a major component of the Iraq reconstruction efforts in the postwar period. Iraq needs to undertake measures to
improve service delivery and economic viability as follows: (i) significant investments in the sector, warranted by the economic losses that an undersupplying
sector creates; (ii) balancing between growing generation capacity and fiscal
performance of operations; (iii) reducing losses and improving sector revenues, as
tariffs and collection rates are well below cost recovery; and (iv) institutional
reform and tariff restructuring, to improve operational performance and financial
self-sustainability.

Notes

1. Republic of Iraq, Ministry of Electricity, Iraq and KRG Electricity Master Plans,
   Parsons Brinckerhoff, December 2010.
2. IEA Iraq Energy Outlook, October 2012; UNDP; and Iraq Report to U.S. Congress,
   October 2011.
3. IEA Iraq Energy Outlook, October 2012.
4. Ibid.
5. Republic of Iraq, Ministry of Electricity, Iraq Electricity Master Plan, Executive
   Summary, Parsons Brinckerhoff, December 2010.
6. UN Iraq Knowledge Network, Essential Services Factsheet, December 2011.
7. Peak demand includes unsuppressed load (that is, demand that would exist if supply
   were unconstrained).
8. IEA Iraq Energy Outlook October 2012; Iraq & KRG Electricity Master Plans 2009–
   10; and World Bank analysis based on "Integrated National Energy Strategy (INES),"
   2012.
9. According to UNDP, public opinion on the quality of electricity supplies declined
   dramatically in 2006 and 2007, with only 8 percent expressing a positive opinion in
   2007. By February 2009, this had recovered to 38 percent. Improved perceptions
   coincided with a slight increase in the proportion of demand being met.
10. Iraq and KRG Electricity Master Plans 2009–10, and World Bank analysis.
11. The proposed pipeline would provide 25 MMCM per day for five years—enough gas
    to generate 2,500 megawatts.
12. In 2009, the MoE entered into the "Mega Deal" with General Electric to purchase 56
    combustion turbines—each with a nameplate capacity of 125 megawatts. Constructions
    for the plants using these turbines began in 2011.
13. In March 2011, the MoE reached an agreement with three foreign firms to install 50
    diesel-fuelled emergency power generator stations (producing 4 megawatts each, add-
    ing a total of 5 gigawatts in capacity) across the country as an interim solution.
14. BP Statistical Review, 2011.
15. EIA Iraq Country Brief, 2012.
16. INES Final Report 2012.
17. Iraq and KRG Electricity Master Plans 2009–10.
18. The line is capable to transmit around 1,000 megawatts, which is about 15 percent of
    the total power supply in the MoE's grid.

19. Iraq and KRG Electricity Master Plans 2009–10 and INES Final Report 2012.

20. Ibid.

21. World Bank analysis; U.S. Congress Iraq Report 2011; and INES Final Report 2012.

22. INES Final Report, 2012.

23. World Bank analysis, and INES Final Report 2012.

24. Iraq and KRG Electricity Master Plans.

CHAPTER 5

Case Study #2: Health

Introduction

Iraq's health sector also suffers from most of the public spending issues discussed in this report. There are serious efficiency and equity issues in the sector, negatively affecting health outcomes. Budget allocation to health spending is low in Iraq compared with other countries, and yet administrative spending is high. In addition, budget execution rates are low, which contributes to inefficiency of service delivery.

Health outcomes have deteriorated as a result of conflict, inefficient service delivery, and poor access to health services. Life expectancy at birth is low, and Iraq faces serious challenges with respect to diseases. There are serious issues related to child health and development and, a significant proportion of children in Iraq are malnourished compared with other countries. The country faces significant development challenges because of poverty and malnutrition. There are large disparities between the rural and urban areas in Iraq, in terms of both poverty incidence and access to social services. Rural poverty incidence is more than twice the rate of poverty incidence in urban areas, and there is at least a 10 percent gap between the rural and urban areas in access to sanitation facilities. Many hospitals also lack health resources and skilled health staff.

This chapter analyzes public spending issues in the health sector on both policy and implementation outcomes, and proposes to undertake a health sector Public Expenditure Review (PER), creating an in-depth review of these issues. While the main challenge is to fund the health sector sufficiently, a detailed review of the sector could provide insights on how increased financing could be used efficiently to provide basic health services. It is important to identify operational inefficiencies in the sector and propose policy options to improve the health care delivery system, quality, and the efficiency of public spending.

An Overview of the Health Sector in Iraq: Health Outcomes, Service Coverage, and Resources

The Iraqi health system has suffered critical damages over the past two decades. Much of the physical infrastructure has been destroyed, many of the competent health staff have left the country, and large sections of the population suffer from serious ill health and disease. The conflict, in combination with international sanctions, has led to major socioeconomic challenges. Poverty, malnutrition, and insecurity are widespread, and despite large oil resources, Iraq today faces a number of economic and human development challenges that will determine much of the policy space for the Government of Iraq (GoI) as it embarks upon health financing and systems reform.

Prior to 1990, Iraq had a reasonably well-performing health system that was able to provide basic and some high-level services to the vast majority of the population. However, starting from the 1990s, as a result of military and domestic conflicts, the health system deteriorated significantly. There are strong indications of governance and accountability issues in the health sector. Various reports note that graft and fraud is ever present, not least in the hospital and pharmaceutical sectors. In contrast to many other countries that also suffer from mismanagement and poor governance, Iraq has significant resources to invest in the sector. Therefore, the challenge is how to use these resources efficiently and how to invest better to provide good quality service delivery with governance accountability.

The demographics of Iraq is changing. The Iraqi population is relatively young; however, population pyramid projections show that over the coming years the population will gradually change and the youth bulge of the early decades of the twenty-first century will give way to an increasingly older population, with subsequent healthcare needs. The projections for 2020 and 2030 are presented in appendix K.

Iraq's life expectancy and mortality rates are deteriorating. In 2000, the life expectancy at birth (LEB) in Iraq was on average 71 years, while in 2011 it had dropped to 68 years. In Iraq, the effects of prolonged military conflict and the impact of international sanctions on child survival are the major reasons for the decrease in the LEB (or at least for the lack of increase at the rate seen in other countries during the same period). Children from newborn up to five years of age have suffered during the past 20 years in Iraq (appendix L).

The adult mortality rates deteriorated due to the presence of violent conflict within the country and the reduced access to health services as a result. In 1990, the probability of an adult dying between 15 and 60 years old was 202 per 1,000 population; however, the ratio increased sharply to 222 per 1,000 population by 2009 (figure 5.1).

Iraq also faces serious challenges with respect to diseases. Tuberculosis prevalence increased from 100 cases in 1990 to 106 cases in 2004, and to 120 cases per 100,000 people in 2007. The reported number of communicable and noncommunicable diseases is presented in appendix M. In 2009, 5,471 pertussis cases, 2,265 mumps cases, 167 cases of rubella, and 30,328 cases of measles were reported in Iraq.

Figure 5.1 Iraq Adult Mortality Rate, 1990–2009

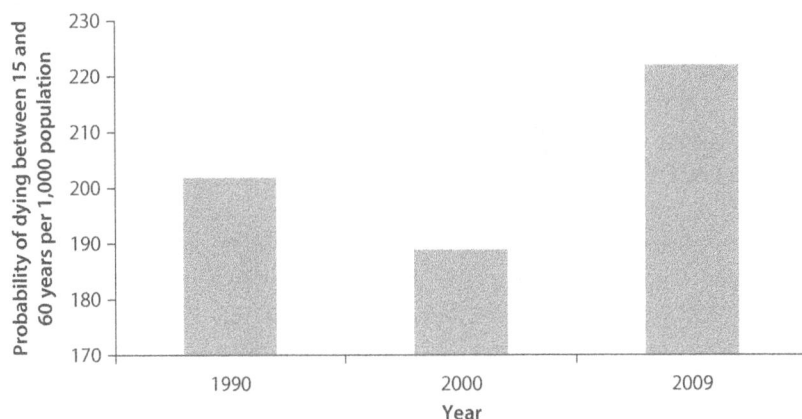

Comparatively, 40 percent of total years of life lost by broader causes in 2008 were attributed to injuries, and 25 percent were attributed to noncommunicable diseases. When compared with the Eastern Mediterranean Region (EMR), the most striking difference in causes of mortality is the high percentage of mortality caused by injuries in Iraq (40 percent) compared to the EMR (14.3 percent).

Data suggest that serious issues related to child health and development persist, and that a considerably larger number of children in Iraq are malnourished, compared with those in other countries.

There is also some indication that many Iraqis suffer from various forms of mental illnesses, such as posttraumatic stress and depression.

The 2010 Board of Supreme Audit Annual Report highlighted that most health centers and hospitals are suffering from shortages. Many hospitals and health centers are suffering from shortage in medicine, medical supplies, and laboratory equipment, while other hospitals experience a surplus and an expired inventory. A lot of laboratory and medical equipment is currently out of order at most hospitals and medical centers. Most health centers and hospitals are also suffering a shortage in doctors, dentists, pharmacists, and other medical cadres. The report also found that health departments inside the borders of the Baghdad Municipality and the provinces failed to achieve any progress in fighting contagious diseases or in implementing inoculating campaigns to prevent them.

The overall deterioration of living standards in Iraq is also reflected in the health services coverage. Evidence suggests that the poor receive lower-quality health care than the nonpoor. Addressing these and other health inequalities is central to the government's reform plans. Immunization is a critical area of importance for population health, and in particular the health of small children. Most countries have been able to either increase or largely maintain previous levels of vaccination coverage. In Iraq, however, coverage rates of all or most key vaccinations have gone down over the past decade. Moreover, although there are considerable gaps in maternal, child, and reproductive health services, available data indicate that there is a decline in number of births attended by skilled personnel (appendix N). Reports from the Iraq government suggest that the majority of health system-related issues require considerable attention to prevent the further decay of health services (World Health Organization [WHO] National Health Account Team for Iraq, 2011).

The lack of health resources and skilled health staff in many hospitals are both important challenges for the Iraqi health system. Over the past decade or so, Iraq has witnessed an exodus of many skilled health workers, with respect to both clinical work and management. Appendix O presents some key health workforce indicators for 2004 and 2009. The relative lack of data makes analysis of the development over time difficult, although many observers agree that the situation with respect to doctors, nurses, midwives, and managers is precarious. The Iraqi population was served by 21,925 physicians in 2009, which translates to a density of 6.9 physicians per 10,000 population. There are 14 nurses/midwives per 10,000 population. In 2009, there were only 13 hospital beds per 10,000 people.

Health Policy in Iraq

The key policy concerns for the Iraqi government are to ensure that public health expenditure provides value for money, and is distributed fairly. Iraq is implementing the Public Sector Modernization (I-PSM) program, which is intended to reform several sectors of the economy in order to improve public service delivery. Along with the education and the water and sanitation sectors, the health sector has been selected as a pilot area for the modernization reforms. The I-PSM is a four-year program, totaling some US$55 million, which targets all levels of the public administration, including the central, governorate, and district levels.

With respect to the health sector, a broad work program is currently being implemented, aiming at identifying the main challenges and options for effective reform in Iraq. Among other aspects, the government is looking at health insurance reform with the aim of universal coverage, enhancing the role of the private sector in service provision, and expanding primary health care. A particular issue in the current reforms is the nature and extent of decentralization of public administration, including the regulation and organization of health services.

The health sector work is being led by the Ministry of Health, and WHO is coordinating development partner activities. It is expected that the World Bank will contribute to the work through analyses and capacity building activities, with a particular focus on the overall policy framework, health financing and insurance, and a review of the public health expenditures.

Efficiency and Equity Issues in Public Expenditure on Health

At around 3–4 percent, health spending as a share of gross domestic product (GDP) is low in Iraq. This is around 2 to 3 percentage points below the average of upper-middle-income countries and 5 to 7 percentage points below the average of most of the high-income Organization for Economic Cooperation and Development (OECD) countries. Most health spending in Iraq is publicly financed.

The effects of both war and political and economic sanctions limited funds available for health spending in the 1980s, burdening an already struggling health system. Additional sanctions in 1990 aggravated further an already-critical situation, and in 1997 select hospitals transitioned away from government funding in favor of patient-funded financing models (World Health Organization Eastern Mediterranean Regional Office [EMRO] 2006). In the years prior to 2003, nearly all health facilities were "off budget" and self-financed by patient payment, with both efficiency and equity implications.

During this period, a significant amount of public expenditure reflected goods from the Oil-for-Food program. The 2003 restructuring reverted the financing scheme back to the original model, which charged only for drugs and curative care. Additionally, the military medical service was included in the Ministry of Health (MoH) in 2003, and as a result the Ministry of Finance provides a large percentage of funding, which covers the costs of salaries, operating expenditures, and pharmaceutical products (EMRO 2006).

The burden of health financing rests on the government and out-of-pocket payments, as Iraq currently does not have a social health insurance system or any significant private health insurance activities (EMRO 2006). However, a small number of companies have offered limited insurance pools for employees. These employer-based insurance schemes dissolved after only a few years, as a result of unsustainable funding.

There is little or no systematic evidence on the effects of the relatively large out-of-pocket (OOP) payments that many Iraqi individuals and households pay to get medical attention. Household survey data, however, suggest that most such payments are spent on pharmaceuticals and outpatient treatments in public and private hospitals and clinics.

As noted, the main source of funding for health in Iraq is general government revenue, primarily through proceeds from the export of oil. These revenues are collected by the Ministry of Finance (MoF), which allocates resources to the MoH among other sectors. The MoH is responsible for the majority of public health services as well as developing sector policies and strategies.

The other significant source of health funding in Iraq is households. In the early part of the period, most health financing was public, and households were required to pay smaller amounts in cost sharing. As a result of military conflict and international sanctions, private health expenditure took on an increasingly more important role. More recently, the country has reverted back to a larger role for public health spending funded by general revenues. Nonetheless, many Iraqis are forced to pay significant amounts out-of-pocket to receive medical treatment (figure 5.2).

With regards to health expenditure as a percent of GDP, Iraq placed last among the set of comparator countries and regions, with an average of 3 percent of GDP. The average for high-income OECD countries was around 11 percent of GDP for the period, the average for the upper-middle-income countries was slightly

Figure 5.2 Private and Public Health Spending, 1996–2011

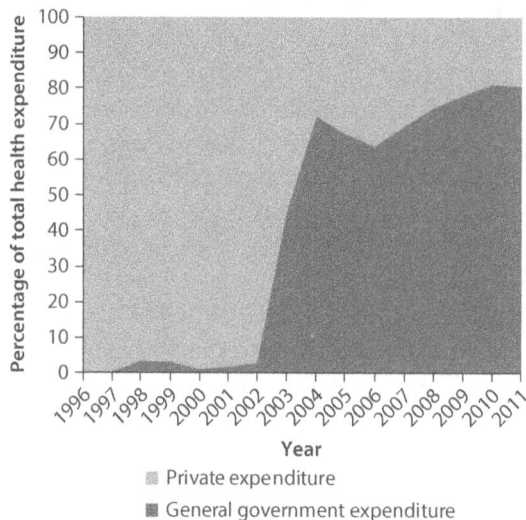

Source: World Bank, World Development Indicators, 2013.

Figure 5.3 Health Expenditure as a Percentage of GDP, 2005–09

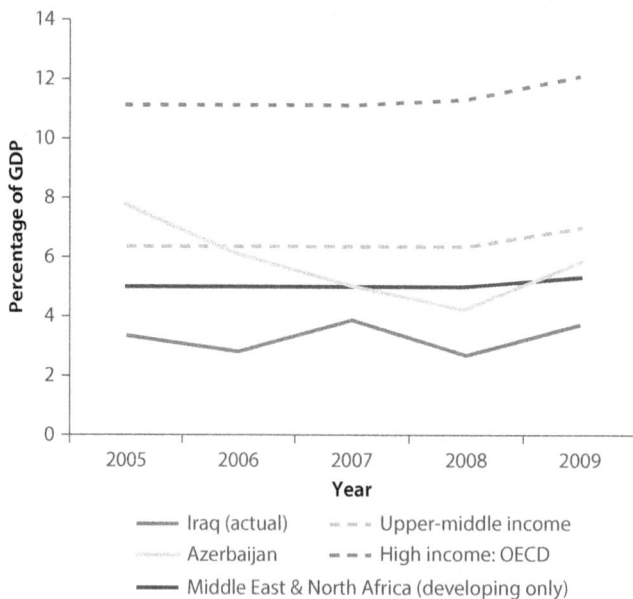

Source: MTFF, 2013–15; World Bank, World Development Indicators, 2013.
Note: OECD = Organization for Economic Cooperation and Development.

above 6 percent and the average for the Middle East and North Africa region countries was around 5 percent of GDP. Among the other resource-rich countries, Azerbaijan varied from 7 to 4.3 percent (figure 5.3). Iraq's health spending trends relative to comparators is presented in appendix P.

At around US$90, Iraq also fared poorly with respect to per capita health expenditure. Whereas Saudi Arabia spent between US$800 and US$1,150 during 2005–09 per capita on health, the average for upper-middle-income countries ranged between US$600 and US$800, and the average for the Middle East and North Africa region countries ranged between US$300 and US$400. República Bolivariana de Venezuela spent between US$500 and US$700, while Azerbaijan spent between US$350 and US$550. Iraq spent between US$40 and US$120 per capita on health over the 2005–09 (figure 5.4).

In addition to fiscal discipline issues, there are operational inefficiencies in the health sector. Iraq's budget execution rates in the health sector have been low. Public health expenditure as a percent of total government expenditure was around 4 percent between 2005 and 2008, with a slight increase to 5.5 percent in 2009.[1] The average for upper-middle-income countries and the Middle East and North Africa regional average was around 9 percent over the 2005 to 2009 period. Compared to other resource-rich countries, Iraq also fares poorly. For example, República Bolivariana de Venezuela and Saudi Arabia also spent around 9 percent of their budget on health expenditures (figure 5.5).

Development assistance in health continues to play a relatively large role for health financing. External resources for health spending were highest in late 1998 and 1999, representing as much as 60 percent of the total expenditure on health (figure 5.6). The heightened availability of external resources for health was

Figure 5.4 Per Capita Health Expenditure, 2005–09

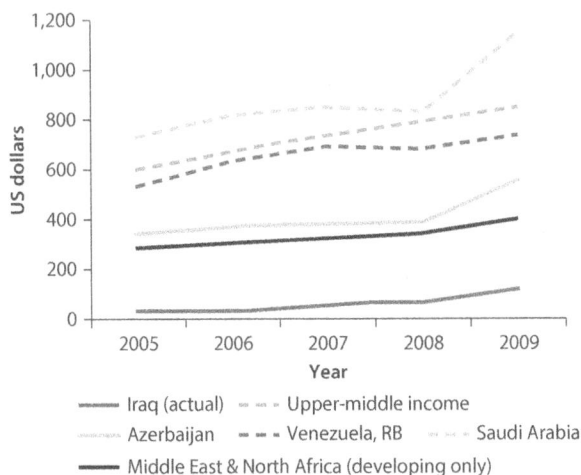

Source: MTFF, 2103–15; World Bank, World Development Indicators, 2013.

Figure 5.5 Health Expenditure as a Share in Total Budget, 2005–09

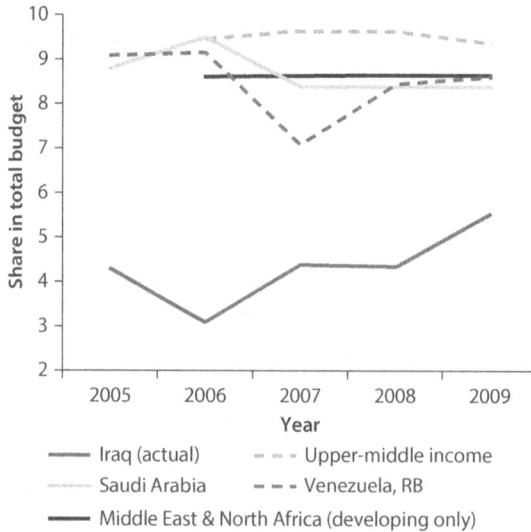

Source: MTFF, 2013–15; World Bank, World Development Indicators, 2013.

Figure 5.6 External Resources on Health, 1996–2011

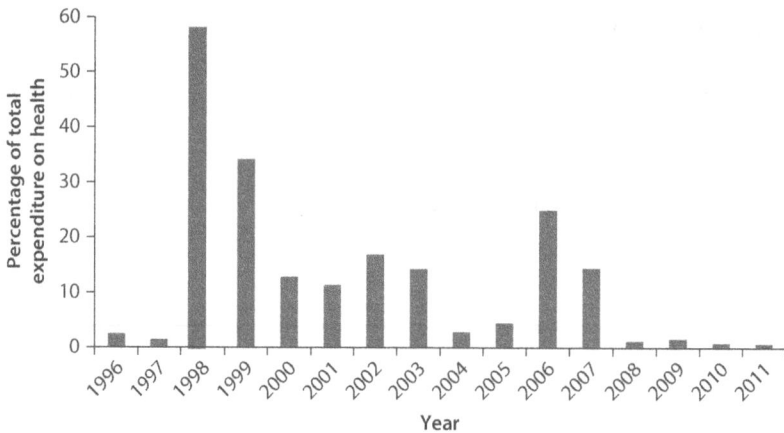

Source: World Bank, World Development Indicators, 2013.

likely due to increased efforts to upgrade and repair existing health facilities by United Nations (UN) agencies and nongovernmental organizations. In the 2000s, the availability of external resources remained below 30 percent of total expenditure on health.

Administrative spending is very high in Iraq, relative to international comparisons. Public health administration consumes 22 percent of total spending, and staff training is only around 1 percent.[2] This issue warrants further analysis, as it suggests significant inefficiencies and related governance challenges.

Health care funding evaluated by function in an Iraq government report on health, indicates that 12 percent is spent on inpatient curative care, 25.5 percent is spent on medical and diagnostic services, and 36.9 percent of the funding is spent on pharmaceuticals and medical nondurables (Iraq NHA Team, 2011). Spending on pharmaceuticals in 2008 amounted to ID 826 billion, or around US$706 million. Additionally, administrative costs account for 22.3 percent, and "health related function" accounts for 3.3 percent (WHO National Health Account Team for Iraq, 2011).

Conclusions and Proposed Work

From the early 1990s to the present, Iraq has experienced prolonged periods of conflict, the implications of which determine the scope for progress and reform, including in the health sector. Further evidence on the value for money and on the equity impacts of health spending in Iraq is needed in order to inform policy making.

Addressing the health challenges discussed above will require substantial investments in new infrastructure, but significant policy changes and improved governance of the Iraqi health system are both equally important. The Government of Iraq will need to increase its health spending, address the issue of underexecution of capital budget, and improve its policy development environment. Reverting the negative trend on health systems performance in Iraq will require significant investments in physical and human resources. It will also require a rethink of the approach to health service provision in Iraq. Finally, it will demand much improved governance and accountability on behalf of all health sector actors.

To assist the GoI implementing its reform programs, the Bank proposes to conduct a Health Sector Public Expenditure Review to help the government to assess the ability of government agencies to deliver health services efficiently and effectively, while maintaining fiscal discipline and strategic prioritization. Operational efficiency will be analyzed depending on the Ministry of Health's interest and demand.

The purpose of this Public Expenditure Review for Health is to inform the health sector policy debate by providing an updated overview and assessment of the Iraqi health financing and services systems. The specific objectives include the following:

- To examine the flow of funds within the public sector, with a public policy focus
- To analyze public recurrent and capital spending on health
- To assess private health spending
- To examine the performance of the health system in service provision and public health
- To enable an enhanced understanding of the key governance and accountability issues within the health sector
- To explore specific aspects and issues of the health sector and related policy areas.

The health sector PER is expected to provide a broad analysis of the Iraqi health system, with an emphasis on health financing and options for reform. The proposed terms of reference for the sector PER are presented in appendix Q. This work could include a series of consultations with the main counterparts and stakeholders. Based on the evidence currently available on the Iraqi economy and health sector, this work will complement that of other policy-related work that is currently being performed or planned.

The Bank team will engage with the Iraqi health sector policy makers and stakeholders across a range of topics. The sector PER will involve the collection and analysis of all relevant and available data on health spending in Iraq, including public (capital and recurrent), private (prepayment and out-of-pocket), and other sources of funding. It will review the nature of health spending over the past years, and will assess the equity, efficiency, and effectiveness of Iraqi public and private health expenditure. The review will also provide an overview of the main epidemiological, demographic, and service delivery issues currently facing the country. Additional activities include a set of policy briefs on issues of particular relevance to the MoH and training events in the area of health financing and system reform. The policy briefs will review the evidence in a particular policy area and present some of the international best practices.

Notes

1. Prior to the 2003 restructuring of the Ministry of Health, execution rate of health budget was even lower than current levels. As a percentage of general government expenditure, health spending was below 2 percent through the 1990s and early 2000s. With integration of military health services and its associated Ministry of Finance funding, expenditure on health increased to 4.4 percent in 2003.
2. WHO National Health Account Team for Iraq, 2011.

Macroeconomic Outlook

	2008	2009	2010	2011	2012	2013	2014e	2015p	2016p	2017p
Economic growth and prices										
Nominal GDP (US$ billion)	89.6	69.2	135.5	180.6	212.5	221.8	238.8	254.0	2 77.6	306.3
Real GDP (% change)	6.6	5.8	5.9	8.6	8.4	3.7	6.3	6.6	8.3	8.9
of which non-oil GDP (% change)	5.4	4.0	9.7	5.7	6.3	4 .0	5.0	6.0	6 .0	6 .0
GDP per capita (US dollars)	2,947	2,215	4,278	5 ,529	6,305	6,377	6,656	6,869	7 ,287	7,812
Oil production (million bpd)	2.3	2.3	2.4	2.7	3.0	3.0	3.3	3.5	3.9	4.4
Oil exports (million bpd)	1.8	1.9	1.9	2.2	2.4	2.5	2.7	2.9	3.2	3.7
Consumer price index (% change)	6.8	-4.4	2.4	5.6	6.1	2.3	5.0	5.5	5.5	5.5
National accounts (in percent of GDP)										
Gross domestic investment	32.2	27.2	21.4	19.3	18.0	19.9	21.3	22.0	22.6	23.1
of which public	30.3	23.7	15.2	13.0	13.5	14.5	14.3	14.2	14.2	14.2
Gross domestic consumption	50.9	91.5	77.9	66.9	73.1	77.5	75.8	75.4	75.6	75.0
of which: public	34.9	55.9	25.2	21.7	21.3	22.7	22.4	22.3	21.9	21.6
Gross national savings	51.0	13.7	24.4	31.8	25.0	20.6	22.2	23.5	24.5	25.2
of which public	29.1	-0.8	10.8	17.7	18.1	14.6	14.4	14.8	15.7	16.6
Saving-investment balance			3.0	12.5	0.7	0.7	0.8	1.5	1.9	2.0
Fiscal and oil sector accounts (in percent of GDP)										
Revenues and grants	82.8	74.5	46.4	49.5	48.2	45.3	44.3	43.1	41.8	42.1
of which oil revenues[a]	70.3	57.9	37.8	44.2	44.2	42.1	41.1	39.7	38.4	38.5
Expenditures	84.1	95.0	50.7	44.6	44.1	46.0	44.6	42.9	40.8	40.1
Operating expenditures	53.8	74.8	35.5	31.6	30.6	31.5	30.4	28.7	26.6	26.0
Capital expenditures	20.6	14.7	15.2	13.0	13.5	14.5	14.3	14.2	14.2	14.2
Overall fiscal balance (including grants)	−1.3	−20.5	−4.3	4.9	4.1	−0.7	−0.3	0.2	1.0	1.9

table continues next page

	2008	2009	2010	2011	2012	2013	2014e	2015p	2016p	2017p
Balance of payments (in percent of GDP unless otherwise indicated)										
Current account balance	12.8	–8.3	3.0	12.5	7.0	0.7	0.8	1.5	1.9	2.0
Trade balance	23.9	–9.5	6.6	18.8	14.8	9.6	9.7	9.2	8.3	8.3
Merchandise exports	69.2	55.5	37.9	44.1	44.3	42.3	41.2	40.0	38.6	38.8
of which oil (in percent of total exports)	*99.5*	*99.7*	*99.6*	*99.7*	*99.7*	*99.5*	*99.5*	*99.4*	*99.4*	*99.3*
Merchandise imports	45.3	65.0	31.3	25.3	29.5	32.7	31.5	30.8	30.3	30.4
External public debt										
Total External debt (US$ billion)	124.2	99.7	60.9	61.0	60.2	27.8	25.5	23.9	22.9	21.9
(in percent of GDP)	*139*	*144*	*44.9*	*33.8*	*28.3*	*12.5*	*10.7*	*9.4*	*8.2*	*7.1*
(in percent of exports)	*179.6*	*179.5*	*118.5*	*76.6*	*64.0*	*29.6*	*25.9*	*23.6*	*21.3*	*18.4*
Memorandum Items										
Iraqi oil price (US$ per barrel)	91.5	55.6	74.2	103.6	106.7	104.5	101.3	95.3	91.2	88.5
Gross reserves (US$ billion)	50.2	44.3	50.6	61.1	70.3	77.8	83.5	89.5	94.4	97.0
Gross reserves in months of imports	*11.2*	*9.5*	*10.6*	*9.5*	*9.3*	*9.9*	*10.3*	*10.2*	*9.7*	*9.1*
Primary fiscal balance (in percent of GDP)	–0.8	–20.0	–3.8	5.6	4.5	0.1	0.3	0.8	1.5	2.4
Exchange rate, ID per US$1 (period average)	1,193	1,170	1,170	1,170	1,166	1,166	—	—		

Source: Iraq authorities and IMF staff estimates.
a. Including revenues of oil-related public enterprises.
Note: GDP = gross domestic product; ID = Iraqi Dinar.

Recurrent and Capital Spending by Administrative Classification, 2005–11

as % of total budget

	2005		2006		2007		2008		2009		2010		2011	
	Recurrent Budget Estimated	Capital Budget Actuals	Recurrent Budget Estimated	Capital Budget Actuals	Recurrent Budget Estimated	Capital Budget Actuals	Recurrent Budget Estimated	Capital Budget Actuals	Recurrent Budget Estimated	Capital Budget Actuals	Recurrent Budget Revised Budget	Capital Budget Revised Budget	Recurrent Budget Original Budget	Capital Budget Original Budget
	(BSA)		(BSA)		(BSA)		(MOF)		(MOF)					
Council of Representatives	0.1	—	0.1	—	0.8	—	0.5	0.0	0.6	0.0	0.6	0.0	0.6	0.0
Presidency	—	—	—	—	—	—	0.3	—	0.2	—	0.1	0.0	0.1	0.0
Council of Ministers	—	0.0	—	0.0	—	—	2.1	0.2	1.7	0.2	1.9	0.8	1.4	0.4
Foreign Affairs	—	0.0	—	0.0	—	—	0.3	0.1	0.3	0.1	0.4	0.2	0.4	0.1
Finance	45.5	6.9	44.5	7.4	20.3	—	39.0	7.5	15.4	0.0	13.2	1.5	15.9	2.0
Interior	—	—	—	0.5	9.8	—	8.1	0.1	10.7	0.3	8.1	0.4	8.0	0.4
Labor and Social Affairs	—	0.0	—	0.0	0.3	—	1.5	0.0	0.5	0.0	0.1	0.0	0.3	0.0
Health	—	0.1	—	0.2	1.6	0.1	4.6	0.1	5.0	0.5	5.4	1.3	5.2	1.4
Defense	—	—	—	1.7	7.3	—	6.7	0.0	6.5	0.1	6.2	0.5	6.3	0.5
Justice	—	0.0	—	0.0	—	—	0.4	0.0	0.6	0.0	0.6	0.0	0.6	0.0
Education	—	0.0	—	0.0	0.0	0.1	5.7	0.2	10.4	0.3	5.9	0.6	5.8	0.6
Youth and Sport	—	0.0	—	0.0	—	—	0.1	0.1	0.1	0.2	0.1	0.6	0.1	0.7
Trade	—	0.0	—	0.0	0.0	—	0.1	0.0	0.1	0.0	5.5	0.1	5.5	0.1
Culture	—	0.0	—	0.0	0.0	—	0.1	0.0	0.2	0.0	0.2	0.0	0.2	0.0
Transportation	—	0.1	—	0.1	—	0.1	0.1	0.1	0.3	0.1	0.5	0.5	0.2	0.5
Municipalities and Public Work	0.8	0.3	1.0	0.3	0.4	0.9	0.1	1.3	0.1	0.9	1.0	1.8	1.0	1.8
Housing & Reconstruction	—	0.2	—	0.2	—	0.4	0.3	0.5	0.3	0.9	0.3	0.9	0.3	0.8
Agriculture	—	0.0	—	0.0	—	—	0.3	0.1	0.3	0.1	0.6	0.2	0.6	0.2
Water Resources	—	0.6	—	0.5	—	—	0.3	1.0	0.4	1.0	0.3	1.3	0.3	1.3
Oil	0.8	0.5	0.6	0.4	1.3	0.9	0.0	6.2	0.1	1.0	1.9	3.6	1.8	3.7
Planning and Development Cooperation	—	0.0	—	0.0	—	—	0.1	0.0	0.1	0.1	0.3	0.1	0.3	0.1
Industry and Minerals	—	0.0	—	0.0	—	—	0.0	0.4	0.2	0.3	0.2	1.1	0.2	0.6

table continues next page

	2005		2006		2007		2008		2009		2010		2011	
	Recurrent Budget Estimated	Capital Budget Actuals	Recurrent Budget Estimated	Capital Budget Actuals	Recurrent Budget Estimated	Capital Budget Actuals	Recurrent Budget Estimated	Capital Budget Actuals	Recurrent Budget Estimated	Capital Budget Actuals	Recurrent Budget Revised Budget	Capital Budget	Recurrent Budget Original Budget	Capital Budget
	(BSA)		(BSA)		(BSA)		(MOF)		(MOF)					
Higher Education	—	0.0	—	0.0	—	—	2.3	0.7	3.2	0.4	2.6	0.5	2.6	0.4
Electricity	14.2	0.7	12.7	0.6	1.2	1.8	0.7	1.2	3.2	1.4	3.3	4.9	3.1	4.9
Science and Technology	—	0.0	—	0.0	—	—	0.1	0.0	0.2	0.0	0.1	0.0	0.1	0.0
Communications	—	—	—	—	—	0.3	0.0	0.1	0.0	0.1	0.1	0.5	0.0	0.4
Environment	—	0.0	—	0.0	—	—	0.0	0.0	0.0	0.0	0.1	0.0	0.1	0.0
Displacement and Migration	—	—	—	—	—	—	0.4	0.0	0.1	0.0	0.2	0.0	0.2	0.0
Human Rights	—	—	—	—	—	—	0.0	0.0	0.0	0.0	0.0	0.0	0.0	0.0
KRG	—	2.5	—	2.0	—	—	8.3	7.3	11.4	4.3	8.2	4.0	8.3	4.3
Directorates unrelated to Ministries	—	—	—	—	—	—	0.6	4.5	1.8	5.1	2.5	3.3	2.3	3.1
Local Councils in the Provinces	—	—	—	—	—	—	0.3	—	0.3	—	0.3	—	0.2	—
Local and General Management in the Provinces	—	—	—	—	—	—	0.2	4.5	1.2	5.1	1.7	3.3	1.5	3.1
Investment commissions at provinces	—	—	—	—	—	—	0.0	—	0.0	—	0.0	—	0.0	—
Iraqi Securities Commission (ISX)	—	—	—	—	—	—	—	—	—	—	0.0	—	—	—
The Independent Supreme Commission for Election	—	—	—	—	—	—	0.1	0.0	0.2	0.0	0.5	0.0	0.5	0.0
Iraqi Criminal Court	—	—	—	—	—	—	0.0	—	0.0	—	0.0	—	0.0	—
Supreme Council of Judiciary	—	0.0	—	0.0	—	—	0.3	0.0	0.4	0.0	0.3	0.0	0.3	0.0
Other	26.5	—	27.1	—	40.1	12.3	0.3	—	—	—	—	—	0.6	—
Total	**87.8**	**12.2**	**85.9**	**14.1**	**83.2**	**16.8**	**83.0**	**17.0**	**82.4**	**17.6**	**70.9**	**29.1**	**71.6**	**28.4**

Source: MTFF, 2013–15.

Note: BSA = Board of Supreme Audit; MOF = Ministry of Finance; — = not available.

Compensation for Employees by Administrative Classification

ID billion

	2005		2006		2007 (BSA)		2008 (MOF)		2009 (MOF)		2010 (MOF)		2011		2012
	Original Budget	Estimated Actuals	Original Budget	Estimated Actuals	Original Budget	Estimated Actuals	Original Budget	Estimated Actuals	Original Budget	Estimated Actuals	Original Budget	Estimated Actuals	Original Budget	Forecast Actuals	Original Budget
Total Compensation for Employees	**4,505**	**5,538**	**8,108**	**8,365**	**10,296**	**13,369**	**12,695**	**17,037**	**21,280**	**21,643**	**23,264**	**20,633**	**28,032**	**24,968**	**29,224**
Council of Representatives	6	43	47	65	110	—	118	125	168	144	193	149	200	189	201
Presidency	9	—	—	25	74	—	22	36	49	43	51	47	64	48	65
Council of Ministers	54	80	94	87	190	—	371	383	490	374	724	605	869	553	873
Foreign Affairs	10	10	12	12	96	—	115	77	165	69	184	123	196	180	219
Finance	27	36	40	39	45	2,870	57	168	103	106	107	117	119	99	120
Interior	595	1,046	2,206	2,201	2,594	3,297	3,679	3,980	5,087	4,844	5,634	4,870	6,179	5,543	7,485
Labor and Social Affairs	27	29	34	35	43	—	51	62	99	81	94	81	100	107	101
Health	398	409	440	427	620	—	1,060	1,583	1,952	2,050	2,177	2,024	2,222	2,171	2,341
Defense	589	839	1,368	1,368	1,801	1,606	1,942	2,100	2,251	2,174	2,553	2,607	3,877	2,540	3,427
Justice	29	41	42	41	62	—	142	153	221	200	261	241	261	246	263
Education	1,103	1,227	1,379	1,375	1,746	—	2,019	3,296	4,403	5,270	4,485	4,327	6,559	6,529	6,124
Youth and Sport	10	13	16	15	19	—	34	24	44	28	41	32	41	42	42
Trade	19	19	22	16	21	—	26	17	31	22	34	22	33	35	33
Culture	19	16	21	19	39	—	47	54	85	66	95	69	96	90	97
Transportation	26	27	29	21	35	—	39	40	38	34	47	40	50	50	50
Municipalities and Public Work	28	30	35	10	15	—	23	26	31	25	40	27	40	34	43
Housing & Reconstruction	43	44	47	42	49	—	55	71	98	92	95	87	97	96	98

table continues next page

	2005		2006		2007		2008		2009		2010		2011		2012
	Original Budget	Estimated Actuals	Original Budget	Estimated Actuals	Original Budget	Estimated Actuals	Original Budget	Estimated Actuals	Original Budget	Estimated Actuals	Original Budget	Estimated Actuals	Original Budget	Forecast Actuals	Original Budget
					(BSA)		(MOF)		(MOF)		(MOF)				
Agriculture	35	37	42	41	54	—	63	108	144	135	148	153	154	150	156
Water Resources	43	48	56	51	64	—	73	115	162	153	170	176	166	160	168
Oil	4	13	7	7	7	—	10	13	22	21	33	43	38	43	38
Planning and Development Cooperation	6	9	9	9	12	—	14	17	31	27	60	35	67	66	68
Industry and Minerals	15	15	16	11	15	—	12	18	23	20	29	22	28	29	29
Higher Education	243	327	474	543	703	—	804	1,226	1,833	1,548	1,749	1,615	1,763	1,749	1,818
Electricity	47	47	48	43	51	—	90	90	176	102	40	72	38	35	38
Science and Technology	28	28	35	34	39	—	46	70	101	92	100	85	105	99	106
Communications	8	8	8	4	6	—	7	7	6	5	8	7	10	12	10
Environment	3	4	5	4	5	—	6	10	20	16	26	18	26	27	27
Displacement and Migration	1	2	2	2	2	—	4	5	6	6	7	6	8	8	8
Human Rights	3	3	3	3	4	—	6	4	8	6	9	6	9	10	9
KRG	1,037	1,049	1,509	1,509	1,500	—	1,500	2,789	2,701	3,406	3,211	2,382	3,870	3,086	4,420
Directorates unrelated to ministries[a]	—	—	—	246	169	—	172	238	316	315	619	402	495	702	498
Supreme Council of Judiciary	40	38	60	60	103	—	92	134	416	172	241	145	248	240	250

a. Represents local councils in the provinces, local and general management in the provinces, investment commissions at provinces, Iraqi Securities Commission (ISX), The Independent Supreme Commission for Election, and Iraqi Criminal Court.

Source: MTFF, 2013–15.

Employment by Ministries and Centrally Funded Departments, 2012

	High a	High b	First	Second	Third	Fourth	Fifth	Sixth	Seventh	Eighth	Ninth	Tenth	Total
1 Council of Representatives	17	47	91	185	343	410	925	1,647	3,566	558	508	321	**8,618**
a. Council of Representatives	10	9	27	26	49	72	125	275	602	145	83	59	**1,482**
b. National Commission for Accountibility and Justice	4	7	12	5	35	47	74	72	100	71	49	37	**513**
c. Property Claims Commission	0	9	10	51	56	75	136	425	428	102	266	143	**1,701**
d. Property Claims Commission - Inspector General Office	0	0	1	2	4	4	5	9	28	7	3	7	**70**
e. Board of Supreme Audit	2	14	22	72	139	126	393	434	1,218	79	48	48	**2,595**
f. Commission of Integrity	1	8	19	29	60	86	192	432	1,190	154	59	27	**2,257**
2 Presidnecy of the Republic	50	22	23	38	41	49	68	77	342	153	124	188	**1,175**
a. Presidency of the Republic	49	22	21	22	32	20	36	50	315	116	118	185	**986**
b. Iraqi Academy of Sciences	1	0	2	16	9	29	32	27	27	37	6	3	**189**
3 Council of Ministers (total)	59	133	178	786	1,367	2,017	3,695	5,931	13,043	4,543	4,795	4,056	**40,603**
a. CoMSec	5	21	31	32	62	114	158	258	320	133	163	122	**1,419**
b. Prime Minister	28	43	25	39	46	65	104	146	466	114	84	172	**1,332**
c. National Security Council	2	12	11	12	19	18	33	41	49	38	43	45	**323**
d. Iraqi Radioactive Source Regulatory Authority	1	1	4	5	11	17	26	26	26	17	15	23	**172**
e. Shiite Endowment	2	13	25	78	289	500	807	1,198	1,687	618	541	773	**6,531**
f. Shite Endowment- Inspector General Office	1	0	1	3	8	4	5	7	21	1	6	5	**62**
g. Sunni Endowment	5	10	15	406	613	921	1,809	2,348	7,005	2,076	1,684	537	**17,429**
h. Sunni Endowment - Inspector General Office	1	0	1	21	18	17	25	16	74	13	11	8	**205**
i. Christian and other religions endowment	1	4	1	7	7	12	15	22	291	15	16	7	**398**
j. Christian and other religions endowment - Inspector General Office	1	0	1	1	3	1	3	8	0	8	3	1	**30**
k. Armed Forces Commander in Chief Office	0	1	2	1	4	7	8	12	17	6	2	3	**63**
l. Iraqi National Intelligence Service	4	13	18	145	197	176	326	1,277	2,319	1,013	2,015	2,004	**9,507**
m. Iraqi National Intelligence Service - Inspector General Office	1	0	1	0	0	2	6	4	32	16	10	20	**92**

table continues next page

	High a	High b	First	Second	Third	Fourth	Fifth	Sixth	Seventh	Eighth	Ninth	Tenth	Total
n. Directorate of militias integration and disarmament	0	1	1	3	6	10	11	12	21	20	8	13	106
o. National Investment Commission	4	7	10	8	16	17	22	47	30	31	11	11	214
p. Imam Adam College	0	2	20	10	40	33	111	121	34	40	52	25	488
q. Imam Kadim College	1	2	5	8	9	9	46	172	152	33	19	68	524
r. Establishment of Martyrs	1	3	4	3	15	88	172	200	464	338	106	213	1,607
s. Establishment of Martyrs - Inspector General Office	1	0	2	4	4	6	8	16	35	13	6	6	101
4 Ministry of Foreign Affairs	189	110	8	148	246	299	649	689	567	196	33	15	3,149
5 Ministry of Finance	2	17	38	297	519	1,576	2,337	1,943	2,325	991	740	381	11,166
6 Ministry of Interior	14	133	211	1,276	3,343	9,070	17,808	29,031	34,291	36,219	69,594	438,495	639,485
7 Ministry of Labor and Social Affairs	5	11	28	330	687	1,164	1,747	1,947	1,891	983	939	676	10,408
8 Ministry of Health	5	24	2,757	6,518	8,686	34,414	33,111	44,500	35,591	30,074	7,061	9,611	212,352
9 Ministry of Defense	90	250	1,318	2,405	4,263	4,025	8,968	12,737	26,166	11,804	125,897	108,691	306,614
10 Ministry of Justice	21	35	27	180	371	908	1,448	1,895	5,280	4,994	10,256	3,027	28,442
11 Ministry of Education	5	41	150	1,978	34,545	48,106	69,153	70,015	186,778	114,064	35,477	40,852	601,164
12 Ministry of Youth and Sports	7	9	16	97	159	272	537	890	2,195	784	708	718	6,392
13 Ministry of Trade	7	9	26	62	252	220	612	602	613	222	118	128	2,871
14 Ministry of Culture	7	19	37	279	603	889	1,719	1,267	1,956	734	484	436	8,430
15 Ministry of Transportation	1	7	12	249	385	388	599	388	985	397	150	27	3,588
16 Ministry of Municipalities and Public Works	4	14	18	182	220	334	675	467	648	251	261	266	3,340
17 Ministry of Construction and Housing	5	12	27	553	552	1,167	2,560	1,627	1,670	908	545	713	10,339
18 Ministry of Agriculture	5	13	14	498	1,393	1,683	2,371	1,437	4,821	1,817	587	724	15,363
19 Ministry of Water Resources	6	23	53	1,232	899	1,826	3,973	2,515	4,237	1,805	522	1,016	18,107
20 Ministry of Oil	8	9	22	63	99	110	173	187	320	128	91	117	1,327
21 Ministry of Planning	5	23	15	194	168	247	351	335	766	222	92	124	2,542
22 Ministry of Industry and Minerals	6	12	13	170	95	111	213	140	39	21	50	3	873
23 Ministry of Higher Education and Scientific Research	31	366	10,346	5,864	6,736	9,824	16,366	18,945	17,383	5,486	3,319	4,476	99,142
24 Ministry of Electricity	9	9	47	110	85	136	184	203	308	180	100	92	1,463

table continues next page

	High a	High b	First	Second	Third	Fourth	Fifth	Sixth	Seventh	Eighth	Ninth	Tenth	Total
25 Ministry of Science and Technology	5	19	106	705	999	1,740	2,316	1,250	2,074	1,015	445	413	11,087
26 Ministry of Communications	6	4	7	19	22	32	53	82	149	36	17	2	429
27 Ministry of Environment	4	11	22	94	143	124	200	245	551	141	88	119	1,742
28 Ministry of Migration and Displaced	5	7	4	16	21	54	84	78	309	135	53	55	821
29 Ministry of Human Rights	4	8	9	29	61	108	195	229	539	102	85	110	1,479
30 KRG	70	996	3,010	11,282	29,368	33,987	48,526	56,769	144,407	121,492	125,712	86,825	662,444
31 Entities not linked to a Ministry (total)	88	174	454	390	703	1,044	2,200	1,964	9,139	6,915	1,552	1,402	26,025
a. Local councils in governorates	0	0	0	15	60	83	131	94	1,363	544	242	325	2,857
b. Public and local departments in governorates	15	119	379	323	489	822	1,638	1,142	3,446	973	659	597	10,602
c. Investment commissions in governorates	0	15	21	32	50	17	21	34	378	136	42	81	827
d. Securities Commission	0	0	3	1	2	3	4	10	33	18	2	16	92
e. The Independent High Electoral Commission	9	38	37	0	70	65	350	513	3,685	5,078	318	154	10,317
f. Iraqi Criminal Tribunal	60	0	1	7	7	36	33	113	103	149	287	212	1,008
g. Mayoralty of Baghdad - Inspector General Office	1	0	3	6	13	9	15	23	45	8	0	17	140
h. Prisoners Foundation - Inspector General Office	1	0	3	3	5	2	2	7	55	8	2	0	88
i. Iraqi General Authority for Broadcasting Services - Inspector General Office	1	0	0	0	2	2	0	0	20	0	0	0	25
j. Hajj and Umrah Commission - Inspector General Office	1	2	7	3	5	5	6	28	11	1	0	0	69
32 Supreme Judicial Council	31	1,466	7	345	244	523	839	1,218	2,270	1,812	318	269	9,342
Grand Total	771	4,033	19,094	36,574	97,618	156,857	224,655	261,250	505,219	349,182	390,721	704,348	2,750,322

Source: World Bank.

Note: CoMSec = Council of Ministers Secretariat; KRG = Kurdish Regional Government.

The Iraqi Budget Process

According to the timetable suggested by Council of Ministers Secretariat (CoMSec) in 2009, by mid-March, the Council of Ministers would need to give final approval to the Budget Priorities Statement and referral to the Minister of Finance in time to prepare and commence the budget cycle, and circulate the budget priorities to all ministries in. In the lead-up:

- Mid-February: Presentation of the Draft Budget Priorities Statement to the Council of Ministers by the Chairman of the Committee, which would also include the presentation of the National Policy Framework
- Mid-February–Mid-March: Review of the Draft Budget Priorities Statement by the ministers and their staff, with due interministerial consultation and detailed review by Ministry of Finance to ensure fiscal sustainability and due process
- Mid-March: Final approval of the Budget Priorities Statement by Council of Ministers, and referral to Minister of Finance in time to prepare budget cycle.

The Section 6 of the Financial Management and Public Debt Law 95/2004 regulate budget preparation process as follows:

During the month of May of each year, the Minister of Finance shall issue a report on the priorities for fiscal policy for the next fiscal year, including the proposed total limit on spending and the limits for each individual spending unit, and submit it to the Council of Ministers for approval, together with the Final Accounts of the Federal Budget as submitted to the Board of Supreme Audit according to section 11(6) of this law, and an update on progress in execution of the budget in the current fiscal year. The Minister of Finance shall consult with the Minister of Planning and Development Cooperation on priorities, estimates of total funding, and procedures for preparing the capital spending plan and current budgetary implications of capital expenditures, including those to be implemented or financed by external sources.

In the month of June of each year, the Minister of Finance, in consultation with the Minister of Planning and Development Cooperation, and based on the priorities for fiscal policy established by the Council of Ministers, shall issue a circular setting guidelines and objectives of fiscal policy for spending units for the preparation of their budgets. The circular shall include key economic parameters, based on the macroeconomic framework, the procedures and timetable for budget preparation, as well as total levels of expenditure for each spending unit. This will serve as the basis for the spending unit to prepare its budget request.

The government priorities are currently prepared by the Deputy Ministers Council and approved by the prime minister. The Budget Strategy Committee, chaired by the Deputy Minister of Finance, is expected to take the priorities into consideration in preparing the budget strategy.

Under Section three of the Constitution, the Council of Ministers (CoM) is required to submit the general budget bill to the Council of Representatives (CoR) for approval. Section 3 also provides powers to the CoR to reallocate proposed budget items. The CoR may recommend that the government increases the total budget. The presidency has the exclusive ratification authority for the annual budget law. Under section three of the Constitution, the Budget Law is considered automatically ratified if 15 days have elapsed after the CoR has transmitted the law to the presidency, and if the presidency has not sent the law back to the CoR for reconsideration.

The Ministries of Finance and Planning issue annual regulations after issuance of the annual budget law. These regulations provide for the financial and accounting rulings and rules for all units starting with financing processes, disbursement, receipt, data preparation, account closure, and submittal of annual and monthly financial statements. The Ministry of Planning issues regulations concerning implementation of government contracts. The projects, which are being implemented under the regional development program, are considered part of the investment activity, and the approved budgetary allocations for these projects are distributed proportionately by population in each province.

The Ministry of Finance consolidates, discusses, and monitors the execution of recurrent revenues and expenditures. On the other hand, the Ministry of Planning prepares and monitors the execution of the capital projects according to the guidelines for the execution of the annual investment budget. Pursuant to the Financial Management Law, the recurrent and investment budgets had been consolidated in the Federal General Budget. The Minister of Finance had been assigned to execute this budget, in consultation with the Minister of Planning. The Ministry of Planning develops the investment approach, and distributes the allocations among ministries and independent agencies. The Ministry of Finance handles the financing process.

Iraq: Strategic Planning Process

Strategic Planning Framework

Legend
- Council of Ministers
- Ministry of Planning
- Ministry of Finance
- Line Ministries
- Governorates

Yearly policy cycle
Feedback/Feed Forward

Boxes (flow):
- Government Priorities
- MTFF
- Ministry Strategies
- Provincial Development Strategies
- Government Programme
- Capital Investment Plan
- Ministry Operational Plans (Indicative)
- Ministry Capital Investment Plans (Indicative)
- Provincial Development Plans (Indicative)
- Budget Strategy
- Unified Budget Circular (Ceilings)
- Final Ministry Operational Plans
- Ministry Capital Investment Plans (Final)
- Provincial Development Plans (Final)
- Budget Submission
- Federal Budget
- Implementation & evaluation

Descriptions (bottom):

Recurring over 4 years and annually: government determines medium-term government priorities every 4 years and annual priorities every year. Impacts of government priorities are reflected in the MTFF.

Recurring Over 4 years: 4-year forward ministry and Government strategies outlining the strategies development objectives of the ministry and governments, based on the government priorities.

Recurring over 4 years: Investment planning. Aligned with government priorities and the available budgetary space indicated by the MTFF macroeconomic forecast.

Recurring over 4 years: The government programme indicates what government intends to do in term of Concrete policies and projects To implement the government Priorities within the 4 years of its electoral team. This include both capital investment and non-capital investment policies. Drafted by COMSec.

Recurring annually, January-April: Spending units prepare their annual Plans of activities, operations and investment for the coming fiscal years, based on the longer term strategies and updated for progress.

Recurring Annually, May: Budget strategy is prepared By MoF in consultation with MoP/Mop provides overview of current budgetary Implications of Capital expenditures. Proposed ceilings are prepared for approval by council of Ministers.

Recurring Annually, June: Financial management law Calls for unified Budget Circular covering capital Investment budget and Operational budget ceilings Prepared by MoF in Cooperation with MoP.

Recurring Annually, July: Spending units finalize their indicative annual plans in line With the budget ceilings in preparation for the budget submission.

Recurring annually, July: Spending units submit their budgets to MoF with capital Investment Section copy to MoP.

Recurring annually, September-October: MoF Submits draft annual budget law to council of ministers and after approval the annual budget law will be sent for approval to the council of Representatives on October 10th.

Recurring Annually, following Fiscal year. Policy implementation and Budget execution throughout the year, followed by evaluations on the results of which influence government priorities.

Source: Adam Smith International (2010). Discussion Paper: 2011 Budget Strategy. Department for International Development.

Note: MTFF = Medium-Term Fiscal Framework.

120

Investment Budget: Advances and Hard Commitments

Spending Unit	Balance of Creditors/Debtor net uncleared advances (+) net hard commitments (−)	2010 Estimated Actuals	% of Estimated Actuals
Council of Representatives	130,130,788	6,451,013,036	2
Presidency	140,425,000	2,028,775,393	7
Council of Ministers	−84,637,188,254	381,511,408,101	−22
Foreign Affairs	120,993,958,282	93,411,853,536	130
Finance	82,387,600	4,732,660,206	2
Interior	24,462,795,916	365,460,148,406	7
Labor and Social Affairs	−181,181,819	15,353,515,761	−1
Health	−2,644,644,874	301,411,958,780	−1
Defense	−36,411,342,123	477,290,460,338	−8
Justice	5,779,500	57,597,263,282	0
Education	14,046,867,465	11,009,179,519	128
Youth and Sport	−42,184,878,778	408,590,000,691	−10
Trade	12,746,753,586	12,238,887,410	104
Culture	−1,366,204,664	23,979,302,665	−6
Transportation	71,640,446,071	120,121,691,267	60
Municipalities and Public Work	147,783,814,718	1,484,252,488,264	10
Housing and Reconstruction	−10,168,757,615	553,720,684,528	−2
Agriculture	18,320,314,173	50,119,271,523	37
Water Resources	115,742,900,246	650,350,999,175	18
Oil	2,181,462,849,605	544,170,067,881	401
Planning and Development Committee	−2,006,003,214	22,648,007,418	−9
Industry and Minerals	278,346,028,711	184,525,101,352	151
Higher Education	−847,911,243	258,358,239,572	0
Electricity	−2,717,395,355,000	3,982,397,025,786	−68
Science and Technology	−206,688,272	13,309,905,667	−2
Communications	58,818,659,346	116,992,848,169	50
Environment	−56,202,920	11,594,576,654	0
Displacement and Migration	3,554,441,608	8,597,743,786	41
Human Rights	−441,678,260	4,225,869,744	−10
Kurdish Regional Government	7,614,000	2,921,403,855,362	0
Supreme Council of Judiciary	2,283,792,791	16,876,049,209	14

APPENDIX H

Total Costs and Annual Appropriations for Transport Projects

(listed after the ratification of 2011 State budget; up to 09/30/2011)

millions of Iraqi dinars

Project	Total cost	Annual appropriations	Ministry	Province
Constructing Ramadi–Nakhib (land road for pilgrimage)	80,000	10,000	Anbar	Anbar
The connecting road (7 km) between Altarmia new bridge and Al-Rashidia road	4,000	1,000	Ministry of Reconstruction and Housing	Baghdad
Constructing country and service road in AL-Qadisya	16,364,147	16,364,147	Diwania Province	Diwania
ALtooz-Tikrit road	36,000	3,000	Ministry of Reconstruction and Housing	Salladin
Implementing the visitors road	65,000	15,000	Ministry of Reconstruction and Housing	Multi
Constructing Karataba–Omar Mindan road and Baghdad–Kirkuk conjunction road (33 km)	8,000	2,000	Ministry of Reconstruction and Housing	Diyala
Constructing the connecting road between AL-Najaf and Kufa cities near the Alnajaf international airport	5,000	5,000	Najaf Province	Najaf
Paving the entrance of highway in Najaf	1,000	1,000	Najaf Province	Najaf
Paving and developing Al-Najaf-Kufa street	5,000	5,000	Najaf Province	Najaf
Implementing the works for the second path and developing Almamal (factory) road in AL-Kufa city	5,000	5,000	Najaf Province	Najaf
The remaining works of the second path project for the two parts of Baghdad–Kirkuk road	3,700	2,500	Ministry of Reconstruction and Housing	Multi
The remaining works to construct AL-Shirqat bridge in Salladin province	1,793	1,500	Ministry of Reconstruction and Housing	Salladin
Muslim Bin Aqeel square and road conjunctions in Kufa city	25,000	250,000	Najaf Province	Al-Najaf

table continues next page

millions of Iraqi dinars (continued)

Project	Total cost	Annual appropriations	Ministry	Province
Updating designs and studies for expressway no. 2	12,000	500	Ministry of Housing and Construction	Multi
Support oil ports	23,243,611	23,243,611	Ministry of Transportation	Basra
Constructing roads and bridges covered by the U.S. grant/the first and second phases	3,748,803	3,748,803	Ministry of Reconstruction and Housing	Multi
Expanding and developing private transportation terminals in Baghdad and the provinces	7,000	60,055	Ministry of Transportation	Multi
Acquisition of lands	15,000	100	Ministry of Transportation	Basra
Connecting Iraq with the neighboring countries (feasibility study)	12,000	438,835	Ministry of Transportation	Baghdad
Baghdad-Baqoba city-Kirkuk-Erbil-Mosul rail line (studies)	10,000	1,000	Ministry of Transportation	Baghdad
Studding Mosul–Zakhoo rail line	8,000	2,191,675	Ministry of Transportation	Baghdad
Studding (Basra-Faw) rail line	4,000	1,000	Ministry of Transportation	Baghdad
Studies and designs (Kirkuk-Sulaimania) (Hamam Al-Aleel-Saboonia) railways	10,000	1,100,053	Ministry of Transportation	Baghdad
Designs of crossroad and the railways	3,000	458,692	Ministry of Transportation	Baghdad
Designs for the railway bridge over Euphrates near Simawa city	1,000	1,303	Ministry of Transportation	Baghdad
Studying Karbala-Ramadi railway	7,000	737,356	Ministry of Transportation	Baghdad
Studies, designs, updating and developing railway construction	3,000	15,355	Ministry of Transportation	Baghdad
Paying costs of the achieved and cancelled railway projects	600	600	Ministry of Transportation	Multi
Constructing two wharfs in Umm Qaser port	33,000	1,055	Ministry of Transportation	Basra
Repairing the travellers' station and maintenance centers in Basra	2,000	1,252	Ministry of Transportation	Basra
Repairing Al-Fihaimy railway bridge	900	165,735	Ministry of Transportation	Basra
Pave 105 km in marshes of Maissan/second phase/ marshes revival	0	4,000	State Ministry of Marshes Affairs	Maissan
Pave 49 km in marshes of Thiqar/second phase/ marshes revival	0	7,000	State Ministry of Marshes Affairs	Thiqar
Pave 22.3 km in Basra marshes/second phase/ marshes revival	0	1,800	State Ministry of Marshes Affairs	Basra
Pave Tar-Hammar-Chibayish road (right Euphrates) 30 km in Thiqar	0	10,000	State Ministry of Marshes Affairs	Thiqar
Pave the road of Bitaira/Ghadeer regulator-Sakhra-Jadi/Mojahideen way 52 km	0	7,000	State Ministry of Marshes Affairs	Maissan

Source: Ministry of Planning.

Estimated Duration of Issuance, Payment, and Clearance of Letters of Credit

Action	Duration	Action	Duration	Approval / Verification
MDA writes contract for goods or services and seeks contract approval	1-4 Weeks	Contracting Committee considers contract	1-4 Weeks	Contracting Committee approves contract

Duration

7 Days

| **L/C Issuance Commencement** MDA requests L/C funding transfer from MoF | 3 Days | | | MoF verifies MDA funds/ appropriations availability |

Duration   Same Week   *3 Days s.t L/C application. issues*

| MDA applies to TBI for L/C | | MoF sends instructions to CBI to transfer of L/C amount the to DFI suspense account for L/Cs and advises MDA *MDA accounts for L/C amount in "Trial Balance" memorandum* | | |

Duration   7 Days   3-7 Days   (Same week)

| TBI writes L/C and sends L/C to JP Morgan | 7 Days | CBI transfers authorized L/C amount the to DFI L/C suspense account | | |

Duration   7 Days   Same week

| FRBNY transfers CBI funds to JP Morgan | 3 Days | JP Morgan Sends L/C to TBI Consortium Member[a] | | |

Duration   3 Days   3 Days

| Consortium Member[a] sends L/C to Vendor Bank (or suppliers account) | 3 Days | Vendor Bank issues L/C to Vendor | 3 Days | Vendor verifies L/C and notifies TBI and MDA of L/C receipt **L/C Issuance Complete** |

Duration   **7 Days**

| Vendor delivers goods or services to MDA *(according to contract terms) MDA accounts for L/C amount in "Trial Balance" memorandum* | xxx Days | **L/C Payment Commencement** Vendor requests MDA to verify delivery of goods or services | 7 Days | Delivery of goods or services verified and accepted by MDA |

Duration   **7-14 Days**

| MDA sends verfied delivery of goods or services documentation to Vendor | **7 Days** | MDA verified documents presented to Vendor Bank by Vendor | **7 Days** | Vendor Bank verifies all required documentation compliant with L/C terms |

Duration   **7-14 Days**

| Vendor receives payment from Vendor Bank | 3 Days | Vendor advises MDA payment from Vendor Bank | | |

Duration   **7 Days**

| MDA accounts for L/C transaction in "Trial Balance" Report | Up to 30 Days | MoF reconciles L/C suspense accounts | 7 Days | MoF confirms with CBI & TBI that L/C suspense accounts cleared (*and requests transfer of balances not used back to MDA account as appropriate*) **L/C Process Complete** |

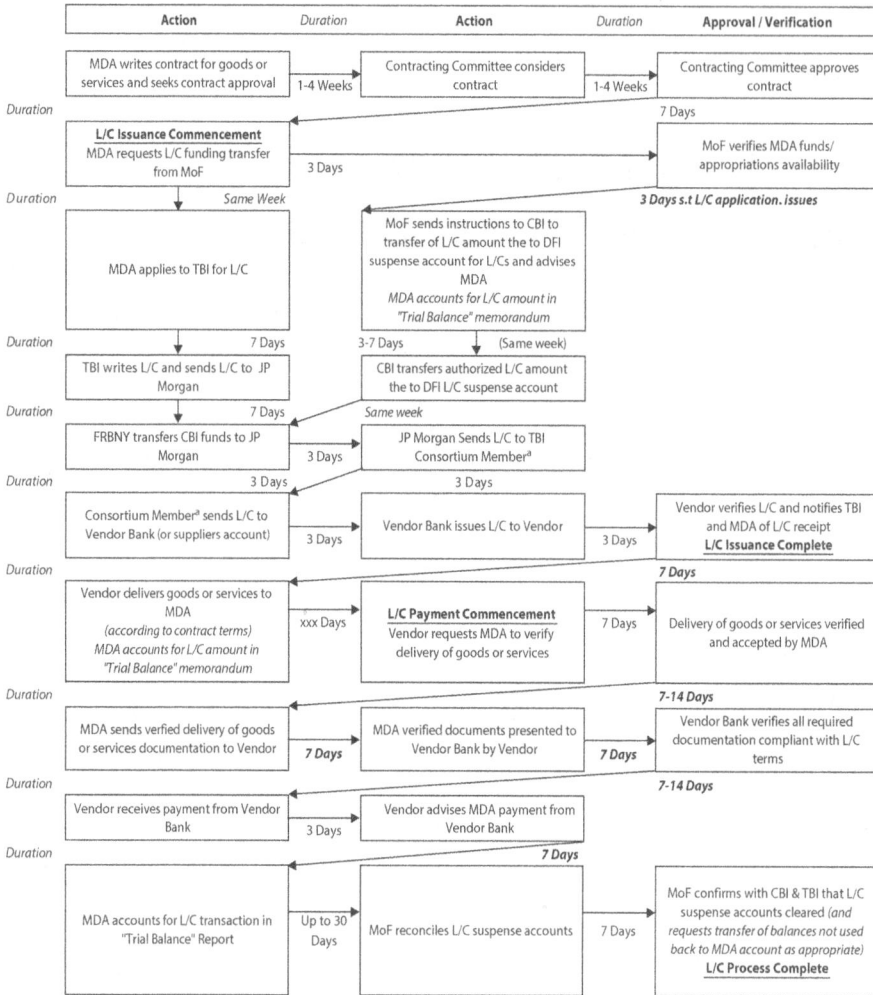

EstimatedL/C Process Duratation	Days
LC issuance	39
LC payment	49
Clearance of L/C suspense accounts	47

a. Consortium members: JPMorgan Chase Bank NA, U.S.A, Standard Chartered Bank, U. A. E, Australia & New Zealand Banking Group Limited, Australia, Bank Millennium SA, Poland, National Bank of Kuwait SAK, Kuwait, ING Bank NV, Netherlands, The Bank of Tokyo – Mitsubishi UFJ Ltd, Japan, Calyon, France, Bayerische Hypo-und Vereinsbank AG (Hypo Vereinsbank), Germany, and Intesa San Paolo SPA, Italy.

Diagnostic Questions for Evaluating Public Investment Efficiency

The following questions might provide the basis for a diagnostic assessment of the efficiency of a public investment management system.

I. Investment Guidance, Project Development, and Preliminary Screening

1. Is there well-publicized strategic guidance for public investment decisions at central/ministerial/provincial levels?
2. Is there an established process for screening of project proposals for basic consistency with government policy and strategic guidance? Is this process effective? What proportion of projects screened is rejected?

II. Formal Project Appraisal

3. Is there a formal appraisal process for more detailed evaluation (whether at line ministry or central finance agency level) of public investment project proposals for costs and benefits? If yes, is appraisal mandatory for all projects or for projects above a certain monetary value? Is project appraisal undertaken only for specific sectors and if so which sectors? What proportion of public investment projects is formally appraised for costs and benefits?

III. Independent Review of Appraisal

4. Are project appraisals formally undertaken by the sponsoring department or by an external agency? What is the quality of such appraisals?

IV. Project Selection and Budgeting

5. What proportion of the Public Investment Program (PIP) is donor financed? Are donor-financed projects subject to the same or different rules for

appraisal and inclusion in the budget as government-financed projects? If different, describe the difference. Does the government review project appraisals undertaken by donors?

6. Are appraisals screened by an external agency or department for quality and objectivity of appraisal?

7. Is final project selection undertaken as part of the budget process or prior to the budget process? Does the government maintain an inventory of appraised projects for budgetary consideration?

8. Is there an effective process to control the gates to the budgeted public investment program, that is, the collection of projects that are formally approved for budget allocation and implementation? Is the number of oversight agencies limited and their key roles clearly specified? Do delegation levels exist for bringing projects to the center? Is there an established but limited process for including projects for emergency or politically imperative reasons?

9. To illustrate, if the residual investment to complete the current program is US$1,000 and the annual investment budget is typically US$100, the completion rate is 10 percent, implying 10 years to complete. A low completion rate may confirm a poor gate-keeping process that allows too many projects into the budget or it may reflect cost escalation that causes the cost of completing projects to exceed initial estimates.

    a. What proportion of projects enter the PIP by "climbing the fence" by avoiding the gate-keeping process?

    b. What proportion of projects that "climb the fence" is donor financed?

10. What is the average the value of new projects relative to the:

    a. Ongoing public investment program?

    b. Projects completed (use three-year moving average)?

V. Project Implementation

11. What is the completion rate of the public investment program (annual average over the past five years), defined as the annual public investment budget divided by the estimated cost to complete the current public investment program? How does this differ across key sectors education, health, water supply and sanitation, roads, and power, for example?

12. Do ministries undertake procurement plans in line with good practice (that is, use competitive tendering)? And, if so, do they implement procurement plans effectively?

VI. Project Adjustment

13. Has the government undertaken a rationalization of its public investment program in the recent past? Did the rationalization improve the prioritization of the public investment program? Did it result in the cancellation or closure of ongoing projects? If yes, what is the percent of the PIP that was

cancelled or closed? Indicate if projects were merely "deferred" rather than cancelled.

14. Are project implementing agencies required to prepare periodic progress reports on projects? Does this include an update on the cost benefit analysis? Are the sponsoring departments accountable for changes recorded in either costs or benefits and for the delivery of net benefits? What mechanisms exist to ensure that this occurs? Is this record of investment management used in subsequent budget discussions with the Ministry of Finance (MoF) or Ministry of Planning (MoP)?

15. For a representative subset of the public investment program (including Bank-supported projects), what is the average percentage cost overrun (in inflation-adjusted terms) on major projects in key sectors?

VII. Facility Operation

16. Are projects commissioned to private contractors and, if so, are contracts awarded on the basis of competitive bidding? Are international firms permitted to bid on contracts? If other methods are used, describe the methods. Is there any evidence from Country Procurement Assessment Reviews (CPARs) or other reviews of procurement contributing to cost escalation or fraud?

VIII. Basic Completion Review and Evaluation

17. Is there a process for handover of management responsibility for future operation and maintenance of the created assets to service delivery agencies? Do service delivery agencies have an adequate budget funding to operate and maintain these assets? Is service delivery associated with facility operation tracked through time? Are agencies held accountable for the delivery of services?

18. Does the government maintain an asset register or inventory of public sector property, equipment, and vehicles ? Is legal title to assets maintained? Are assets valued according to sound accounting principles, such that the accounting definition of an asset is met, depreciation is deducted from the asset value and where feasible, asset values are updated to reflect changed prices?

19. For a representative subset of the public investment program, what is the delay in project completion relative to initial estimated time and what is the deviation from the original (and amended) budget on major projects in key sectors?

20. Is the actual net present value (NPV) of completed projects measured, and is a project end evaluation undertaken to review the nature of differences relative to the estimated NPV at appraisal? What alternative methods, if any, are used to undertake ex post evaluation of completed projects?

The Population Pyramids: 1990, 2020, and 2030

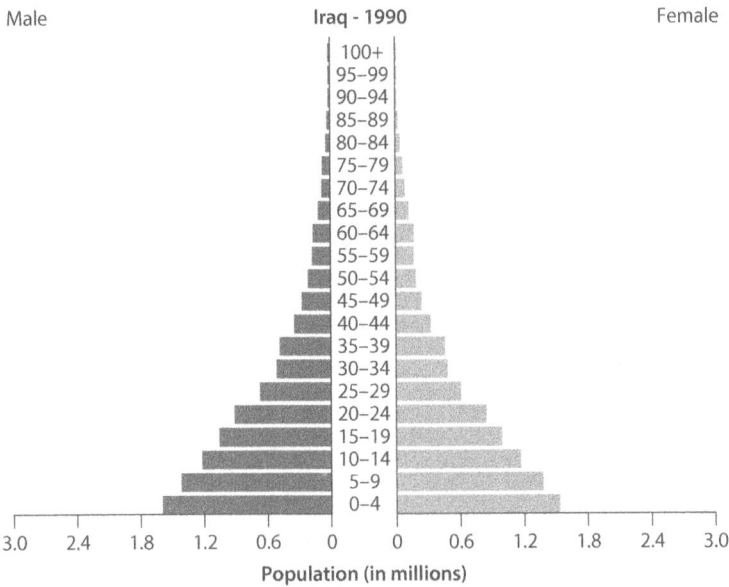

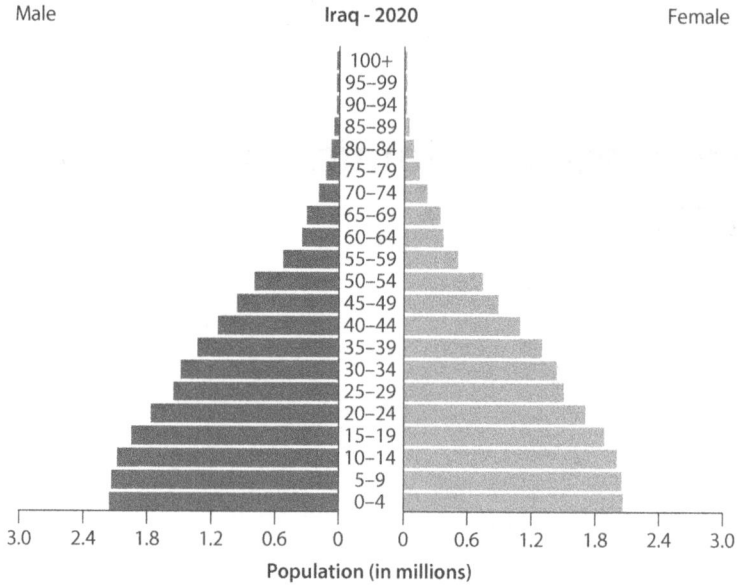

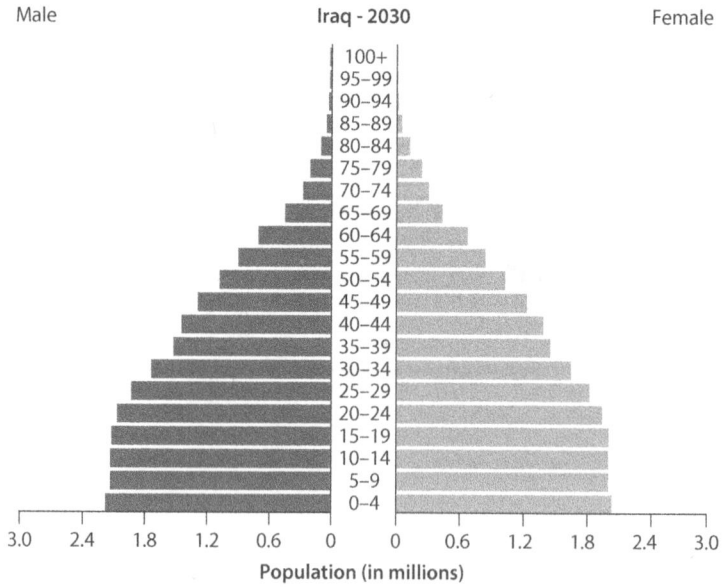

Republic of Iraq Public Expenditure Review • http://dx.doi.org/10.1596/978-1-4648-0294-2

Iraq Infant and Child Health Indicators

	1990	1995	2000	2005	2006	2008	2009
Stillbirth rate (per 1,000 total births)							9
Neonatal mortality rate (per 1,000 live births)	26	24	24	23			23
Low-birth-weight newborns (%)					15		
Neonatal tetanus—number of reported cases							17
Infants exclusively breastfed for the first six months of life (%)					25		
Children aged <5 underweight (%)			12.9		7.1		
Children aged <5 stunted (%)			28.3		27.5		
Children aged <5 years overweight (%)			5.5		15		
Distribution of causes of death among children aged <5 years (%)—pneumonia						21	
Distribution of causes of death among children aged <5 years (%)—injuries						5	
Distribution of causes of death among children aged <5 years (%)—diarrhea						13	
Distribution of causes of death among children aged <5 years (%)—other						17	

Iraq Communicable and Noncommunicable Diseases

	2008	2009
Communicable Diseases (number of reported cases)		
Diphtheria		13
Pertussis		5,471
Total tetanus		34
Malaria		1
Mumps		2,265
Cholera		6
Rubella		167
Measles		30,328
Distribution of years of life lost by broader causes (%)—communicable	35	
Noncommunicable Disease		
Distribution of years of life lost by broader causes (%)—injuries	40	
Age-standardized mortality rate by cause (per 100,000 population)—injuries	280	
Distribution of years of life lost by broader causes (%)—noncommunicable	25	
Age-standardized mortality rate by cause (per 100,000 population)—noncommunicable	691	

Maternal, Child, and Reproductive Health Care Services

	2000	2006	2007
Maternal Health			
Births attended by skilled health personnel (%)		89	79.7
Civil registration coverage of births (%)		95	
Births by caesarean section (%)	35		
Child Health			
Children aged <5 years with acute respiratory infection symptoms taken to a health facility (%)		81.6	
Children aged <5 years with diarrhea receiving ORT (%)		30.7	
Reproductive Health			
Contraceptive prevalence rate (%)		49.8	
Population aged 15–24 years with comprehensive correct knowledge of HIV/AIDS, female (%)		3	

Health Workforce and Resources

	2004	2009
Health Workforce		
Number of physicians		21,925
Physicians density (per 10,000 population)		6.9
Number of nursing and midwifery personnel		43,850
Nursing and midwifery personnel density (per 10,000 population)		13.8
Number of dentistry personnel		4,766
Dentistry personnel density (per 10,000 population)		1.5
Number of community health workers	149	
Community health workers density (per 10,000 population)	0.06	
Number of pharmaceutical personnel		5,401
Density of pharmaceutical personnel (per 10,000 population)		1.7
Number of environment and public health workers	2,601	
Density of environment and public health workers (per 10,000 population)	1	
Health Resources		
Hospital beds (per 10,000 population)		13

Iraq Health Spending and Comparators

	Total expenditure on health as a percentage of gross domestic product		
	2000	*2004*	*2008*
Iraq	1.4	5.2	2.7
MENA average	4.99	5.25	5
Lower-middle income	4.5	4.5	4.4
Global average	9.2	10.0	9.6
	General government expenditure on health as a percentage of total expenditure on health		
	2000	*2004*	*2008*
Iraq	28.7	80.7	81.2
MENA average	57.735	60.84	61.96
Lower-middle income	37.1	38.3	44.0
Global average	57.8	58.9	60.4
	General government expenditure on health as a percentage of total government expenditure		
	2000	*2004*	*2008*
Iraq	1.3	3.4	3.1
MENA average	8.02	8.29	8.685
Lower-middle income	7.8	7.6	8.0
Global average	14.5	15.5	15.2
	Private expenditure on health as a percentage of total expenditure on health		
	2000	*2004*	*2008*
Iraq	71.3	19.3	18.8
MENA average	42.265	39.16	38.04
Lower-middle income	62.9	61.7	56.0
Global average	42.2	41.1	39.6

table continues next page

	Out-of-pocket expenditure as a percentage of private expenditure on health		
	2000	2004	2008
Iraq	100.0	100.0	100.0
MENA average	84.455	84.095	86.02
Lower-middle income	93.2	90.5	90.7
Global average	44.6	42.4	45.2
	Private prepaid plans as a percentage of private expenditure on health		
	2000	2004	2008
Iraq	0.0	0.0	0.0
MENA average	8.96	9.04	8.865
Lower-middle income	2.6	4.9	5.5
Global average	43.9	46.7	44.2
	Social security expenditure on health as a percentage of general government expenditure on health		
	2000	2004	2008
Iraq	0.0	0.0	0.0
MENA average	13.39	14.26	11.685
Lower-middle income	37.8	36.8	38.1
Global average	47.6	43.0	41.0

Note: MENA = Middle East and North Africa.

Terms of Reference for the Proposed Health Public Expenditure Review

A key objective of the proposed Health Sector Public Expenditure Review (PER) exercise is to provide the Ministry of Health with relevant information and analysis to assist in the preparation and implementation of the health sector budget. As such, the following information would be collected and analyzed:

Recurrent Expenditures

The review will include an assessment of the following sources:

- Official documents setting out written statements of government policy regarding public expenditure on health
- Samples of the relevant financial reporting forms and guidelines for reporting procedures used both at the institutional level and at different levels of government
- Relevant government documents setting out the budget norms per facility and per capita which are used in allocating recurrent expenditures on health, and any supporting studies of operations and maintenance requirements relevant to setting these budget norms.

In addition, a database on actual public expenditure on the health sector over the past three to five years, and planned expenditures for 2010–11 would be developed.

These data would include those expenditures which are financed by external aid through the state budget, and would cover at minimum:

- **Total public expenditures** on health sector for the central and governorate level; public/private health spending as share of total health expenditure; out-of-pocket expenditure as share of total private health expenditure and total health expenditure
- **Allocation of expenditure** by program: breakdowns between the standard program categories as reported in official budget statistics that is primary, secondary, and tertiary

- **Composition of expenditure** by type of input: breakdowns of recurrent expenditure between standard line items as reported in official budget statistics that is, salaries, materials, pharmaceuticals, maintenance, and other
- **Distribution of expenditure** by governorate: breakdowns both for local government expenditure and for central government expenditure.

Investment Expenditures

Investment expenditures are available from the Ministry of Finance's annual budgets and spending reports. Based on this information, the following analysis would be conducted:

- The extent of physical completion of each project and how much money is required to complete the project would be estimated.
- For each of the governorates, the 3–5 projects which are of the highest and the lowest priority would be defined and resource allocation decision proposed accordingly.
- The capital investment program would be prepared to ensure that it matches the sector's strategic priorities.

Estimation of Administrative Cost of Running the Investment Budget

Recurrent budget requirements would be estimated for operating the existing facilities, and operating the facilities coming on stream over the next three years.

Cost Sharing and User Fees

Any cost sharing arrangements would be analyzed along the following:

- Official documents setting out government policy governing the imposition of fees, and the reporting and use of revenues by state-owned health facilities
- Policy objectives underlying the introduction of fees charged for publicly provided health services, and the rationale for its structure (that is, generating revenues, encouraging efficiency, and improving equity)
- The actual level and structure of prices paid by users of public facilities. The price data would cover the full range of official and unofficial charges, including, but not restricted to, user fees, pharmaceutical expenditures and private provision of basic medical supplies.
- Exemptions and criteria are applied to determine eligibility for the exemption. These characteristics of the pricing structure would be documented separately for each of the main different levels of health services.

- The overall level of revenues generated by user charges for publicly provided health services. The cost recovery ratio for different types of health facilities would be assessed.

Data sources to be considered would include:

- Routine budget reporting systems of MoF and MoP.
- Financial reports filed by individual health institutions.

Bibliography

Adam Smith International. 2009a. "Reforming the Government of Iraq Budget Strategy." Discussion Paper No. 1, Department for International Development.

———. 2009b. "Preparing the Government of Iraq Budget Strategy, 2010." Discussion Paper No. 2, Department for International Development.

———. 2009c. "Linking Priorities and Resources, 2010." Discussion Paper No. 3, Department for International Development.

———.2010. "2011 Budget Strategy." Discussion Paper, Department for International Development.

———. 2011a. "2012–14 Budget Strategy." Discussion Paper, Department for International Development.

———. 2011b. "Iraq: Fiduciary and Development Risk Assessment." Review of Fiduciary and Development Risks, 2007–10.

———. 2011c. "Iraq—Fiduciary and Development Risk Assessment." Technical Working Paper, Department for International Development and Swedish International Development Cooperation Agency.

Alkhoja, Ghassan, and Zaina Dawani. 2011. "Pension Reform Implementation Support Technical Assistance PRISTA: Institution Building in Iraq—The PRISTA Model." MENA Knowledge and Learning Quick Note Series Number 50, World Bank, December.

Araujo, Jorge Thompson. 2010. *Harnessing Oil Wealth for Long-Term Economic Development in Iraq: The Role of Fiscal Policy.* Washington, DC: World Bank.

Auty, Richard M. 2001. "Resource Abundance and Economic Development." Oxford University Press.

Beschel, Robert, Bill Monks, Mikhail Pryadilnikov, and Catherine Laurent. 2007. "The Imperative of Wage Containment & Payroll Reform." Policy Note, World Bank, Washington, DC.

Beschel, Robert, and David Biggs. 2009. "Civil Service Reform in the KRG." Policy Note, World Bank, Washington, DC, August.

Collier, Paul. 2007. *The Bottom Billion—Why the Poorest Countries Are Failing and What Can Be Done about It.* Oxford: Oxford University Press.

Collier, Paul, and Benedikt Goderis. 2007. "Commodity Prices, Growth, and the Natural Resource Curse—Reconciling a Conundrum." Working paper, WPS/2007–15, Centre for the Study of African Economies, University of Oxford.

Concept Note for a World Bank Technical Assistance on "Iraq: Rationalization of the Universal Public Distribution System Technical Assistance," November 2010.

Devarajan, Shantayanan, Tuan Minh Le, and Gaël Raballand. 2010. "Increasing Public Expenditure Efficiency in Oil-Rich Economies: A Proposal," World Bank Policy Research Working Paper No. 5287. World Bank, Washington, DC.

Dunia Frontier Consultants. 2010. "Foreign Commercial Activity in Iraq." Washington, DC.

———. 2011. "Iraqi Commercial Activity and Business Development Opportunities." Washington, DC, August.

Economist Intelligence Unit. 2012. Iraq Country Report, April.

Gupta, Sanjeev, Marjin Verhoeven, Robert Gillingham, Christian Schiller, Ali Mansoor, and Juan Pablo Codoba. 2000. *Equity and Efficiency in the Reform of Price Subsidies: A Guide for Policy Makers*. International Monetary Fund: Washington, DC.

Gylfason, Thorvaldur and Herbertsson, Tryggvi Thor and Zoega, Gylfi. 1999. A Mixed Blessing: Natural Resources and Economic Growth. Macroeconomic Dynamics 3, 204-25.

Integrated National Energy Strategy for Iraq. 2012.

International Energy Agency. 2012. Iraq Energy Outlook.

International Monetary Fund. 1991. *Public Expenditure Handbook: A Guide to Public Policy Issues in Developing Countries*. Edited by Ke-yung Chu and Richard Hemming.

International Monetary Fund Working Paper. 2010. "Investing in Public Investment: An Index of Public Investment Efficiency." December.

Iraq Agriculture Sector Note. 2011. Paolo Luciani with contributions by Maurice Saade. Prepared under the Food and Agriculture Organization of the United Nations and the World Bank. FAO Investment Center.

Iraq Electricity Master Plan. 2009.

Iraq National Health Accounts. 2011. Ministry of Health, World Health Organization, and United Nations Development Programme.

Iraq Public Sector Modernization Program. 2011. Key Findings and Recommendations: Education, Health, and Water & Sanitation, *Draft I-PSM Document*. UNDP, WHO, UNESCO, UNFPA, UNESCWA, UNICEF, UN HABITAT with the support of the European Union.

Iraq Report to US Congress. 2011. October.

Iraq Task Force for Economic Reforms. 2010. With the assistance of the United Nations and the World Bank. Roadmap for Restructuring State Owned Enterprises in Iraq. Baghdad, Iraq, August.

KRG Electricity Master Plan. 2009.

Lederman, Daniel, and Maloney William. 2007. *Natural Resources Neither Curse Nor Destiny*. Stanford, CA: Stanford University Press.

Leite, Carlos, and Jens Weidmann. 1999. "Does Mother Nature Corrupt? Natural Resources, Corruption, and Economic Growth." IMF Working Paper No. 99/85, International Monetary Fund, Washington, DC.

Moore, Pete, and Christopher Parker. 2007. The War Economy of Iraq. Middle East Research and Information Project.

Potter, Barry and Jack Diamond. 1999. *Guidelines for Public Expenditure Management*. International Monetary Fund: Washington, DC.

PricewaterhouseCoopers. 2011. "Iraqi Extractive Industries Transparency Initiative (IEITI: Reconciliation of Cash Inflows from the Petroleum Industry in Iraq in 2009." December.

Rajaram, Anand, Tuan Minh Le, Nataliya Biletska, and Jim Brumby. 2010. "A Diagnostic Framework for Assessing Public Investment Management." Policy Research Working Paper WPS 5397, World Bank, Washington, DC.

Republic of Iraq Board of Supreme Audit. 2010. Annual Report Summary. May.

———. 2011. Summary of the Annual Report for 2010. April.

Republic of Iraq Ministry of Electricity. 2010. "Iraq and KRG Electricity Master Plans." December.

Republic of Iraq Ministry of Planning, Government Investment Program Department. 2011. "Investment Budget and Actual Expenditure." September.

———. 2011. "Problems and Obstacles of Implementing Investment Projects."

Sachs, Jeffery, and Warner, Andrew. 1995. "Natural Resource Abundance and Economic Growth." NBER Working Paper No. 5398.

Sachs, Jeffery, and Warner, Andrew. 2001. "The Curse of Natural Resources." *European Economic Review* 45.

UNDP Electricity Sector Factsheet. 2011.

UNDP Iraq Knowledge Network Survey. 2011.

USAID Electricity Regulation Paper. May 2005.

World Bank. 1998. "Public Expenditure Management Handbook." Washington, DC.

———. 2006. "Rebuilding Iraq: Economic Reform and Transition." Washington, DC.

———. 2007. *Fiscal Policy and Economic Growth: Lessons for Eastern Europe and Central Asia*. Edited by Cheryl Gray, Tracy Lane and Aristomene Varoudakis.

———. 2008. "Public Expenditure and Institutional Assessment Volumes I and II." Washington, DC.

World Bank. 2010a. "Confronting Poverty in Iraq." An Analytical Report on the Living Standards of the Iraqi Population.

———. 2010b. "Intergovernmental Fiscal Management in Iraq: Challenges and Options for a Petroleum-Dependent Economy." Policy Note, June.

———. 2010c. "Intergovernmental Fiscal Management in Natural-Resource Rich Settings: A Guide for Policy Practitioners." June.

———. 2011. "Addressing Governance Challenges in the Short and Long Term." Iraq Governance Policy Note, September.

———. 2012. "2013–15 Budget Strategy." Discussion Paper.

World Bank Aide Memoire on Rationalization of the Public Distribution System Technical Assistance, June 2011.

World Bank Concept Note. 2011. "Iraq Programmatic Country Economic Memorandum: Managing Oil Revenues." January.

World Bank Concept Note for a Technical Assistance. 2010. "Iraq: Rationalization of the Universal Public Distribution System Technical Assistance." November.

World Bank Iraq Electricity Sector Policy Note, September 2009.

World Bank Iraq Governance Policy Note, December 2011.

World Bank Middle East and North Africa Region Health Sector Team. 2011. A back-
    ground paper on "Health Financing and Systems Reform for Performance and Equity"
    by Bjorn Ekman. September.

World Bank Middle East and North Africa Region Energy Team. 2011. A background
    paper on "Issues and Opportunities in the Iraqi Electricity Sector" by Ferhat Esen,
    Simon Stolp, and Husam Beides. December.

World Health Organization EMRO. 2006. "Health System Profile: Iraq." Regional Health
    Systems Observatory.

Environmental Benefits Statement

The World Bank is committed to reducing its environmental footprint. In support of this commitment, the Publishing and Knowledge Division leverages electronic publishing options and print-on-demand technology, which is located in regional hubs worldwide. Together, these initiatives enable print runs to be lowered and shipping distances decreased, resulting in reduced paper consumption, chemical use, greenhouse gas emissions, and waste.

The Publishing and Knowledge Division follows the recommended standards for paper use set by the Green Press Initiative. Whenever possible, books are printed on 50 percent to 100 percent postconsumer recycled paper, and at least 50 percent of the fiber in our book paper is either unbleached or bleached using Totally Chlorine Free (TCF), Processed Chlorine Free (PCF), or Enhanced Elemental Chlorine Free (EECF) processes.

More information about the Bank's environmental philosophy can be found at http://crinfo.worldbank.org/wbcrinfo/node/4.

green
press
INITIATIVE

www.ingramcontent.com/pod-product-compliance
Lightning Source LLC
Chambersburg PA
CBHW082356270326
41935CB00013B/1642